APR 0 8 2003

P9-DHS-103

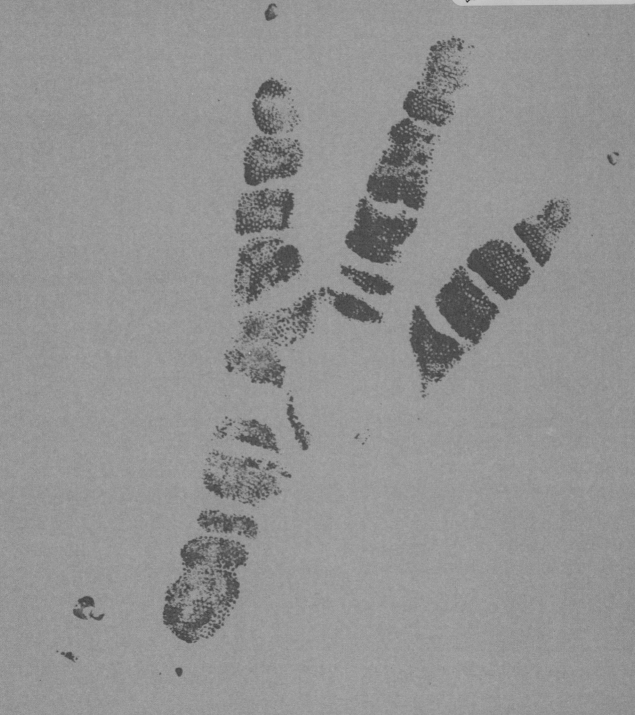

Dodo

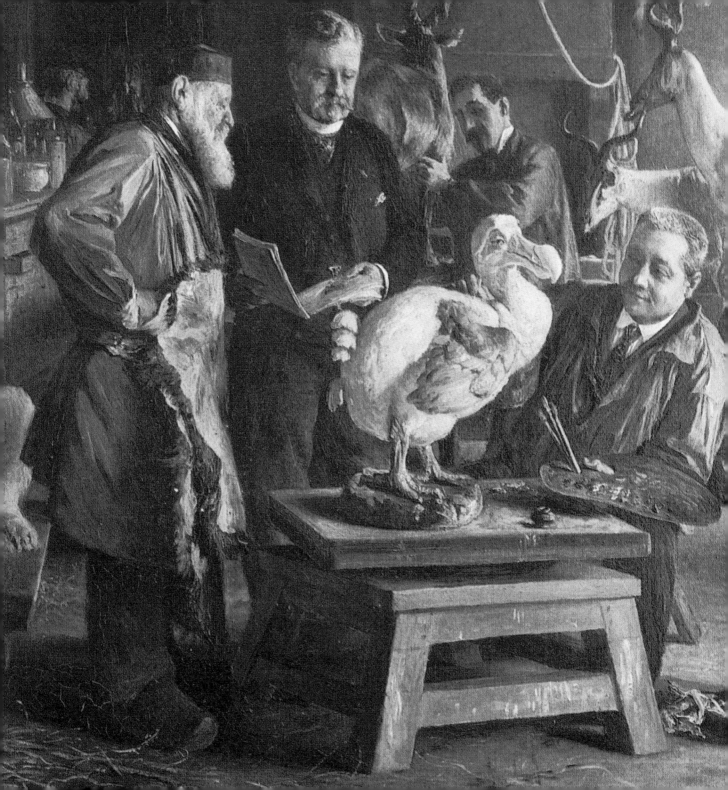

Dodo

A Brief History

WITHDRAWN

BLOOMINGDALE PUBLIC LIBRARY
101 FAIRFIELD WAY
BLOOMINGDALE, IL 60108
630 - 529 - 3120

Errol Fuller

UNIVERSE

First published in the United States of America in 2002
by UNIVERSE PUBLISHING
A Division of Rizzoli International Publications, Inc.
300 Park Avenue South
New York, NY 10010

Distributed to the U. S. trade by St. Martin's Press, New York

This book was produced by Collins
Collins is an imprint of Harper Collins Publishers Ltd.
www.collins.co.uk

© 2002 Errol Fuller

The author asserts his moral rights to be identified as the author of this
work. All rights reserved. No part of this publication may be reproduced or
transmitted in any form or by any means, electronic or mechanical, including
photocopy, recording or any information retrieval system, without permission
in writing from the publisher.

ISBN: 0-7893-0840-1

Color reproduction by Colorscan, Singapore
Printed and bound by Johnson Editorial Ltd., Italy

for Sue

FRONT COVER
A dodo. Chromolithograph by F. W. Frohawk from W. Rothschild's Extinct Birds *(1907).*

ENDPAPERS
Dodo footprints, actual size, created by Rungwe Kingdon.

HALF TITLE
Design in pencil by Alfred Waterhouse (1830–1905) for a panel over a doorway in the southeast gallery of the Natural History Museum.

FRONTISPIECE
Reconstructing the Dodo in the Studio of Professor Oustalet, *1903. Oil on canvas by Henry Coelas. Muséum National d'Histoire Naturelle, Paris.*

PAGE 5
A view of Mauritius.

PAGE 7
Dodo memorabilia.

PAGE 8
The Dodo solemnly presented the thimble. *Coloured engraving for Lewis Carrol's* Alice's Adventures in Wonderland *by Sir John Tenniel (1865).*

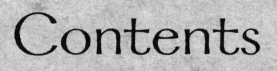

Contents

Prologue

*First here only...is generated the **Dodo**, which for shape and rareness may antagonize the **Phoenix** of **Arabia**: her body is round and fat, few weigh less than fifty pound. It is reputed more for wonder than for food, greasie stomackes may seeke after them, but to the delicate they are offensive and of no nourishment. Her visage darts forth melancholy, as sensible of Nature's injurie in framing so great a body to be guided with complementall wings, so small and impotent, that they serve only to prove her Bird.*

*...Her eyes are small and like to **Diamonds**, round and rowling; her clothing downy feathers, her traine three small plumes, short and inproportionable, her legs suiting to her body, her pounces sharp, her appetite strong and greedy.*

SIR THOMAS HERBERT (1634)

Introduction

Dodo is a strange word. And unlike most words it has a meaning that operates on two levels. First, of course, it means a bird of a certain kind, but second it symbolizes dead, gone, vanished, failed, extinct. The dodo is one of the great icons of extinction. Indeed, it is the ultimate icon. Only *Tyrannosaurus rex* or perhaps some of the sauropod dinosaurs can run it close. In the Dutch language dodo is an anagram of *dood* – which means dead. In English the expression 'as dead as a dodo' is universal, something that even young children understand. Clearly, its widespread use owes much to its alliterative appeal but also this usage has something to do with the bird's popularity and celebrity. Certainly, at least part of this celebrity is due to the name. Dodo is so short, so repetitive, and so curiously catchy that once heard it is unlikely to be forgotten.

The bird too is memorable. Its appearance was quite unlike that of any other. The massive beak, large head, great bulk and strange tail cause it to stand out from the crowd.

Then there is the story. Discovered by mariners in the last decade of the sixteenth century it was all but gone some forty years later. While individuals may have lingered here and there for some decades longer, the species was a spent force within just a few years of European arrival on its island refuge. It is probable that some living individuals reached Europe where, presumably, they caused something of a stir. It may be that some of these *emigres* even outlived their Mauritian counterparts. Who knows? Perhaps, the very last dodo of all died thousands of miles from its homeland.

Yet for all its celebrity there is a strange paradox that surrounds the dodo. Despite its enormous popularity and the great proliferation of dodo literature, we know almost nothing about the bird itself. But of one thing we can be sure. There are now no dodos.

PAGE 10
The Last Flight of the Dodo. *Stained glass panel by Benjamin P. Finn*

OPPOSITE PAGE
The Dodo. *Oils on canvas by Johannes Savery (1650). Oxford University Zoological Museum.*

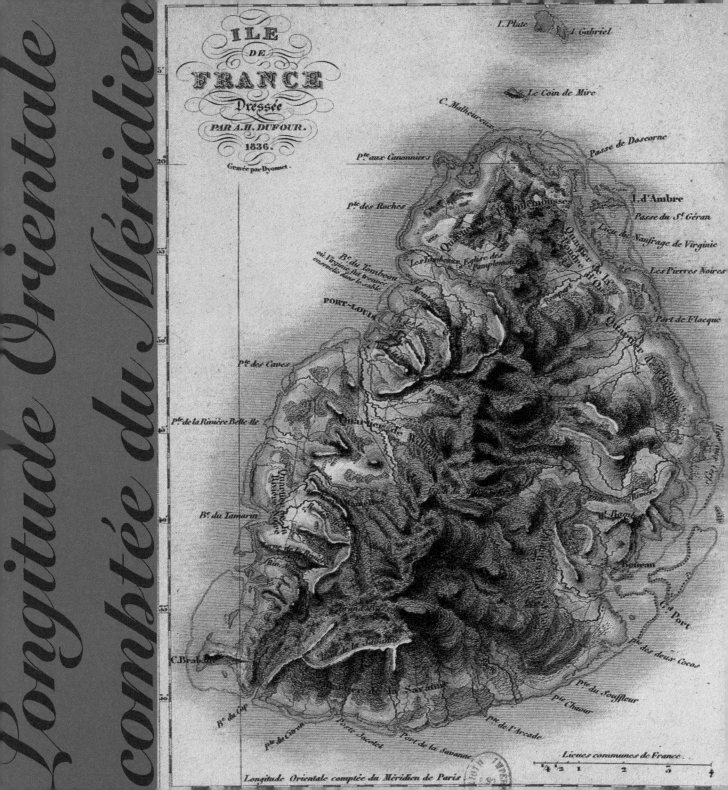

ILE DE FRANCE

Dressée

PAR A. H. DUFOUR.

1836.

Gravée par Dyonnet.

I. Plate   I. Gabriel

Le Coin de Mire

C. Malheureux

Passe de Doscorne

Pte aux Canonniers

Pte des Roches

I. d'Ambre

Passe du St Géran

Lieu du Naufrage de Virginie

Pamplemousses

Bie du Tombeau
où Virginie fut trouvée
ensevelie dans le sable

Les Tombeaux Eglise des
Pamplemousses

Les Pierres Noires

PORT-LOUIS

Port de Flacque

Pte des Caves

Pte de la Rivière Belle-Ile

Quartier de Moka

Bie du Tamarin

Quartier Rivière Noire

V. Bang

Bruneau

C. Brabant

Gd Port

Pte des deux Cocos

Pte du Souffleur

Pte Chaour

Quartier de la Savanne

Pte de l'Arcade

Bie du Cap

Pte du Cirne

Poste Jacotet

Port de la Savanne

Lieues communes de France

¼ ½ 1   2   3

Longitude Orientale comptée du Méridien de Paris.

A Brief History

of the Dodo

A Brief History of the Dodo

PAGE 14
An old map of Mauritius.

BELOW
Part of the Dutch fleet returning to Holland (1599). Oils on canvas by Hendrik Cornelisz Vroom. Amsterdam Historisch Museum.

In the year 1598, during the month of September, ships from Holland under the command of Vice-Admiral Wybrant van Warwijck drew close to the shores of Mauritius. Their coming spelled doom for the dodo. No-one knows quite how long the process of extinction took but it followed close on the heels of the arrival of Europeans. Perhaps it took 40 or 50 years, perhaps a few years longer. What seems certain is that by the year 1690 – and probably decades earlier – there were no dodos left alive.

In the short period of time during which the dodo came into regular contact with man a few records and notes of its existence were made, both in written and pictorial form. And then it was gone, leaving behind some scattered physical relics: skeletal remains that would be retrieved from swamps some two centuries after the bird's demise, a stuffed specimen that was destroyed long ago and a few other sundry fragments.

Although we can be sure it was the influence of man that caused the dodo's downfall, we have no way of knowing how the species was faring on the previously uninhabited island. Perhaps it was already rather rare or localized at the time of European arrival. What evidence there is suggests that dodos inhabited areas close to

the coast rather than the deeper interior. Mauritius is a large and rugged island (some 40km x 60km) and it seems unlikely that extinction could have been accomplished quite so rapidly had dodos occupied all the remoter areas. After all, there were comparatively few people on the island during the seventeenth century and although the animals they brought – monkeys, cats, rats, pigs – were running riot and undoubtedly contributed to the dodo's extinction, it is unlikely that these creatures would have infested the entire island in so short a space of time.

It is known that Mauritius was visited by Arab vessels several centuries before the Dutch arrived and Portuguese sailors had also chanced upon the island. It is clear that the Portuguese were in the habit of visiting from time to time and they seem to have discovered Mauritius during the first decade of the sixteenth century, almost a hundred years before the coming of the Dutch. A certain Pedro Mascaregnas is credited with being the discoverer and from his name is derived the name Mascarenes, which covers the three islands in the group, Mauritius, Réunion and Rodrigues. The Portuguese named Mauritius itself Cerne (Swan) Island and some have held that this is because they saw dodos there and were reminded of swans.

No Arab record makes any mention of dodos, however, and the Portuguese were notoriously secretive about any discoveries they made. It is sometimes speculated that there may be, lying overlooked in a Portuguese archive, some unknown record that relates to dodos, but so far none has turned up. As far as we can tell, neither Arabs nor Portuguese made much impact on the dodo population (although it is conceivable

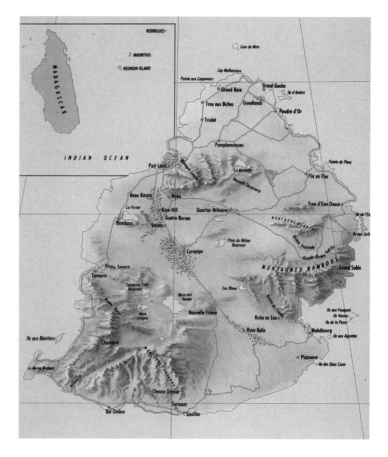

Mauritius – a modern map.

that they left behind mammalian predators which may have been making inroads into numbers well before the arrival of the Dutch).

There is some evidence to suggest that the word dodo is, in fact, of Portuguese origin. *Duedo*, *doudo* or *doido*, a Portuguese word meaning idiot, has been suggested as one likely root for the name. Another possible origin might be Dutch – *dodaersen* could be translated as 'fat behinds' and a second Dutch word, *dronte* – which has apparently fallen into disuse but perhaps meant swollen – is

sometimes held to have been corrupted into dodo. A third Dutch word that perhaps has a connection is *dodoor*, which means a sluggard. 'Dodo' may, of course, be simply a phonetic rendering of the bird's cry although there is no real evidence for this. It would not be an unlikely call for a cooeing pigeon-like bird.

However the word dodo originated, records of the bird that have survived to the present day began with the Dutch invasion of Mauritius. It is perhaps more correct to describe this as a European invasion rather than a purely Dutch one for there were Germans, French and other nationalities aboard the trading vessels that the Dutch commanded. Unfortunately, the records and the seventeenth century illustrations that depict the species are, in many respects, contradictory in the image that they build up and, despite the seeming wealth of evidence, we may never know exactly what the dodo looked like and how it behaved.

Peering back from a distance of four centuries, it is quite clear that dodos immediately intrigued the sailors who found them. The main concern of these men was certainly a dietary one and a bird as large as the dodo was bound to cause culinary interest. When sailors landed on Mauritius they had been at sea for many weeks and the fresh meat of the dodo – or, for that matter, any other creature – must have seemed very appetizing. Yet the accounts of this particular meat vary. Some found it tasty, others found it disgusting. The strange name *walghvogel*, which was sometimes applied to the species, means 'disgusting bird'. Perhaps the most insightful remarks on the gastronomic delights of the dodo come from the pen of the English courtier Sir Thomas Herbert, who

RIGHT
A reconstruction of the coming of Europeans and their animals painted for a children's book on extinction, I Wonder Why the Dodo is Dead *(1996).*

FACING PAGE
The frontispiece to Richard Owen's celebrated (but excessively rare) Memoir on the Dodo *(1866). Hand-coloured lithograph by James Erxleben. The three images are copied from three seventeenth century paintings by Roelandt Savery.*

wrote in incomparable prose:

Greasie stomackes may seeke after them, but to the delicate they are offensive and of no nourishment.

This is probably as near to the truth as we shall ever get and is perhaps another way of expressing the old adage, 'hunger is the best sauce'.

Despite the chief attraction lying in the matter of food, there is no doubt that those encountering dodos on Mauritius found them intriguing in other ways. They aroused sufficient interest for the visitors to send living specimens back to Europe and also onwards to places further east. The English traveller Peter Mundy seems to have seen two individuals in Surat, India where the Mogul Emperor Jahangir kept a menagerie. Others were seen in Batavia (Djakarta). Stories that dodos reached Japan may or may not be true. As far as Europe is concerned, there is no reason to doubt that a number of living specimens arrived. Curiously, however, there is only one piece of hard evidence, and that is for a bird living in London around 1638 and famously reported by a certain Sir Hamon

L'Estrange. He penned a long account of this creature beginning in the following words:

About 1638 as I walked London streets, I saw the picture of a strange looking fowle hung out upon a cloth and myselfe with one or two more in company went in to see it.

One of the strange things about dodo literature is that a number of writers have tried to deduce the precise number of dodos that reached Europe alive and each has come up with entirely fanciful figures based on the most minimal – even non-existent – evidence. Similarly, on perceived differences in some of the existing seventeenth century paintings they (most particularly Hachisuka, 1953 and Oudemans, 1917) have even tried to prove that several different species of dodo existed and reached Europe, and vainly attempted to

FACING PAGE
Paradise. *Oils on canvas by Roelandt Savery (1626). Gemäldegalerie, Staatliche Museen zu Berlin.*

FAR LEFT
detail from Paradise.

LEFT
dodo head (detail from Dodo and Hoopoe*). Watercolour by Cornelius Saftleven (1638). Boymans Museum, Rotterdam.*

determine sexual differentials. The established fact that a stuffed specimen was most definitely in Prague during the first decade of the seventeenth century has been wrongly used as evidence that it arrived there alive. The truth is that most of the surviving paintings (by Savery, Hoefnagel etc.) could have been produced using live birds as models or, more likely, they were painted from crudely stuffed examples. On the other hand, a wonderful picture by Cornelius Saftleven, now in the Boymans Museum, Rotterdam, was almost certainly painted from a living creature. To anyone used to looking at or painting birds, the jaunty attitude is most suggestive of a living individual. Yet this particular picture is rarely mentioned by ornithological dodologists.

No-one knows what parts of Mauritius were inhabited by dodos. Traditionally it has been assumed that the birds were found close to the coast, and what evidence there is points clearly to this. The Mare aux Songes, a swampy area from which almost all the surviving bones were recovered, is close to the sea and most of the written reports concerning encounters with dodos seem to suggest that the birds occurred near to the water or on islands close to the shore. Julian Hume, an English painter and writer, has made an exhaustive study in Mauritius of dodo localities and believes it likely that dodos occupied the coastal strip on the west and south of the island, which area enjoys a rather dryer climate than other parts. The truth is that we shall never really know, of course.

There are many myths that have sprung up in the literature concerning the natural history of the dodo, some of which are endlessly repeated as hard fact. To account for discrepancies in written descriptions and

pictures it is regularly suggested that dodos had a fat season and a thin one and that these differences were clearly discernible to the naked eye. Some bird species do indeed have a very considerable seasonal weight variation but the phenomenon is a measurable rather than a visual one. It is hard to think of a single avian species in which weight loss can be determined by eye alone. The kakapo (*Strigops habroptilus*) of New Zealand has been suggested, but even in this extreme case it is doubtful if the differential is clearly visible. This factor then can hardly be used to account for any differences in seventeenth century paintings and writings. It is far more likely that such differences can be explained by grossly over-stuffed specimens being used as models, or by artistic licence. Nor is the idea that captive dodos were fattened up a sound one. A caged wild creature cannot usually be turned into a fat one. Such domesticating processes occur over generations of captivity so the idea that Dutch painters produced pictures of obese – and artificially – plumpened creatures is therefore a weak one.

Another erroneous idea that is often repeated comes from the work of S. A. Temple (1983) who argued that the hard seed of an upland high canopy tree known as the tambalacoque (*Calvaria major*) could only germinate if passed through the gut of a dodo. This highly unlikely proposition gained something of a following despite its sheer illogicality. Young tambalacoques have been sprouting throughout the twentieth century and they have certainly been doing this without help from dodos.

What is actually known of the living, breathing dodo is minimal. It seems to have lived in groups – perhaps quite large ones – and at least one report maintains it lived on fruit. It seems probable that it also foraged along the shore for shellfish and various products of the sea in the way that some other largish pigeons do.

For pigeon this bird was. Extraordinary though this concept might at first seem, there is no doubt (on anatomical evidence alone) that this was indeed a gigantic, flightless pigeon.

Once man had begun to colonize Mauritius the dodos' days were strictly numbered. By 1640 – just four decades after the Dutch arrived – the species was barely clinging to existence. Rats, cats, pigs and monkeys – both accidentally and deliberately introduced – were swarming over parts of the island and, presumably, presented a particular threat to young dodos and eggs. The adults, with their enormous beaks, were probably well able to look after themselves but chicks must have been especially vulnerable. Dodos were probably able to move quite quickly if they chose but their experience of predators was strictly limited and they would have been completely unprepared for the onslaught of man. The records are quite clear about one thing: he had little difficulty in catching the birds wherever he found them.

The last record of living dodos is variously given as 1662 or 1681. There seems to have been some difficulty over terminology and as the species became increasingly scarcer the name dodo was transferred to another flightless Mauritian bird, the Mauritius red rail or hen (*Aphanapteryx bonasia*). This curious creature was doomed just as surely as the dodo, but it may have survived for a few years longer. The name transferral is something of a controversial subject but assuming it did indeed take place then, quite

*The kakapo (*Strigops habroptilus*), a rare parrot from New Zealand. The species undergoes extreme fat and lean periods, but because of its feathering this phenomenon is not a visible one. Chromolithograph by J. G. Keulemans from W. Buller's* A History of the Birds of New Zealand *(1887-8).*

naturally, it clouds all late records.

Traditionally, the last dodo record is one made by a certain Benjamin Harry, who in 1681 was first mate on a ship named the *Berkley Castle*. However, Anthony Cheke, a specialist in early records relating to the island of Mauritius, believes that the last genuine notice of the dodo comes from the year 1662 when Volkert Evertszen saw birds on a small offshore island. There are some grounds for supposing that this record may be of the rail but at this distance in time such matters cannot be satisfactorily resolved.

Once the living bird was gone there followed a lacunae in dodo research for more than 150 years. Bits and pieces were published and new pictures were issued – but these were based largely on the seventeenth century ones; a few antiquaries noticed the pitifully few dodo relics that existed here and

RIGHT
Aphanapteryx bonasia, the red rail, or hen, of Mauritius. Drawing in ink by an anonymous hand in the journal of the Dutch ship Gelderland (1601). The drawing extends to the extreme right edge of one of the pages.

FACING PAGE
Two views of a dodo head sculpted by Nick Bibby and cast by Pangolin Editions, Chalford, Gloucesterchire.

there.

In 1755 the only surviving stuffed dodo was found to be in such a decrepit state that it was ordered out for destruction. It was part of the collection of the Ashmolean Museum, Oxford and one of the statutes (statute number eight) read:

That as any particular grows old and perishing the keeper may remove it into one of the closets or other repository; and some other to be substituted.

Regarding this statute it can be fairly said that the requirement of 'some other to be substituted' was an impossibility. The bulk of the dodo was consigned to the flames but a certain Mr William Huddersfield, who had just joined the staff of the museum, is supposed to have been responsible for saving the specimen's head and right foot. These pitiful fragments still exist at the University Museum of Zoology, Oxford to which they were long ago transferred from the

ABOVE
A memorial to the dodo on a site at the Mauritius International airport. This site is said to be the Mare aux Songes. In fact, it is not. The real Mare aux Songes is about 2 kilometres away.

RIGHT
The real Mare aux Songes.

FACING PAGE
Dodo Glade. *Acrylic on panel by Julian Hume. Reproduced by kind permission of the artist*

FACING PAGE
*The decorated front and
back covers (showing a
dodo and a Rodrigues
solitary) of H.E.
Strickland and A.G
Melville's* The Dodo and
its Kindred *(1848).*

BELOW
*A fake 'stuffed dodo',
made by the Rowland
Ward Company, typical
of those seen in many
museums around the
world.*

Ashmolean. There is a little background to the origin of the specimen. It came from the celebrated Tradescant collection and there has long been a suspicion that it may have been the very bird that Sir Hamon L'Estrange saw around 1638. There is not a shred of evidence (other than geographical probability) that this is the case, however. There is some evidence to show that there were once several stuffed dodos in Oxford but the clues are unclear and it is difficult to know what to make of them. Perhaps all that can be meaningfully said is that man's desire to hoard up curiosities knows few bounds.

The next significant date in dodo history is the year 1865 when a schoolmaster, Mr. George Clark became interested in the dodo and decided to investigate an area of swamp near the south coast of Mauritius called the Mare aux Songes, close to what is now the international airport. This place still exists despite the fact that many writers have claimed that the airport runways were built over it. The actual locality is, in fact, a kilometre or two from the airport development. It is from the Mare aux Songes that almost all surviving dodo skeletal material originates. Although others have found dodo bones, it is Clark's finds that have provided the bulk of

the study material available today and it is from this rich cache that almost all anatomical studies are derived.

Anyone delving into dodo literature should beware. Most of it is poorly written, badly conceived and contradictory. By far the best work on the dodo is, curiously, the very first book that was published on the subject, H.E. Strickland and A. G. Melville's *The Dodo and its Kindred*. Produced in 1848 (long before most of the skeleton was available for study), it is a model of scientific rigor and is the only dodo book that can be fully relied upon. It is a strange fact that this truly pioneering work remains far and away the most valuable and accurate work on the subject despite the passage of more than a century and a half since its publication.

Finally, a few words might be added about the 'stuffed' dodos that are seen in museums around the world. Many people come away from a museum visit convinced that they have seen a genuine stuffed dodo. They haven't. Despite the realistic appearance, all are fakes made up from the feathers of other birds. Most of the older – and better – ones were, in fact, made up by the Rowland Ward Company of Piccadilly, London, a firm of taxidermists that flourished from the last decade of the nineteenth century until the 1970s. Rowland Ward's wasn't the only outfit to make good fake dodos, however, as is proved by the existence of a wonderful painting by Henry Coelas (*see* frontispiece) called *Reconstructing the Dodo in the Studio of Professor Oustalet* (1903). Oustalet, incidentally, was a celebrated ornithologist who worked at the Muséum National d'Histoire Naturelle, Paris, and had a particular interest in extinct birds.

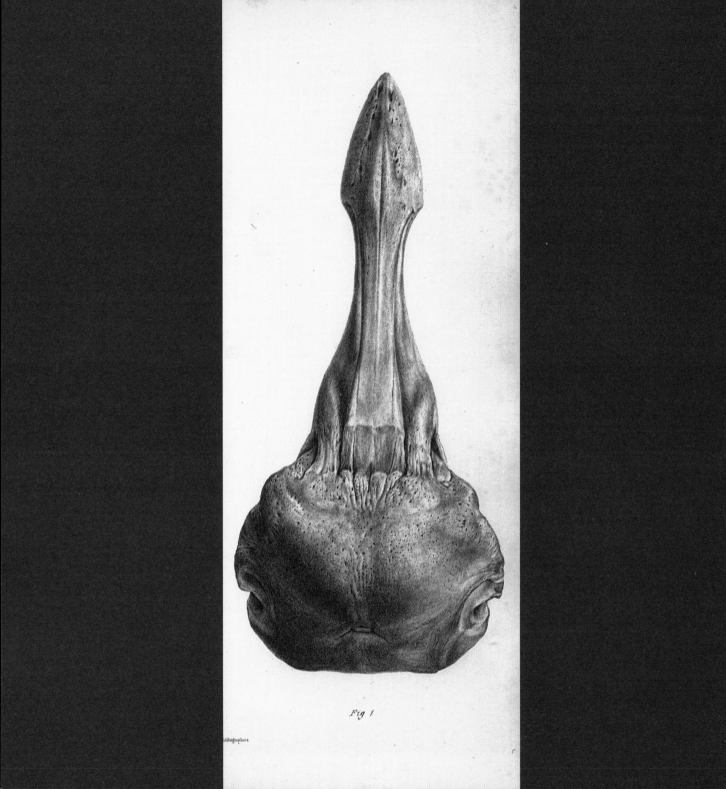

Fig 1

dither graphers

Dodo Natural History

*Dodo skull from above.
Lithograph from H.E.
Strickland and A. G.
Melville's* The Dodo and
its Kindred *(1848). The
skull taken from the
head of the Oxford dodo
served as a model for*

this picture.

*Three distant relatives of
the dodo.*

ABOVE
*Tooth-billed Pigeon by J.
Erxleben from R.
Owen's* Memoir on the
Dodo *(1866).*

RIGHT
*The Liverpool Pigeon
(Caloenas maculata).
Hand-coloured
lithograph by J. Smit
from the* Bulletin of the
Liverpool Museum
(1898).

FAR RIGHT
*Nicobar Pigeon
(Caloenas nicobarica).
Hand-coloured
engraving by Pauline
Knip from* Les Pigeons
(1809–11).

Dodo Natural History

That the dodo was a gigantic pigeon there can be no doubt. Strange and contradictory though this may seem, the proofs are irrefutable. Its closest living relative appears to be the Nicobar pigeon (*Caloenas nicobarica*) from the Indian Ocean and the South Pacific. This pigeon is in itself rather strange and aberrant with no particularly close living relation – although there is an extinct one. This is the mysterious Liverpool pigeon (*C. maculata*) a species known from just a single specimen collected from an unknown locality in the late eighteenth century. Other species that show some distant relationship to dodos appear to be those of the genus Goura, the birds known as crowned pigeons that come from New Guinea. A small but interesting species from Samoa in the Pacific, shows the potential for a pigeon to evolve into something dodo-like. This is the tooth-billed pigeon (*Didunculus strigirostris*) which sports a beak that in shape seems somewhere between that of a regular dove and that of a dodo.

Dodo from extinction to icon

FACING PAGE
*The Victoria Crowned Pigeon (*Goura victoria*), another species that may be related to the dodo.*

LEFT
John Theodore Reinhardt (1816-82).

BELOW
A two day old chick of a pink pigeon (an extant Mauritian species) showing the remarkable similarity of pigeon squabs to the adult dodo. Drawing by Rungwe Kingdon.

The first person to recognize – during the early 1840s – this affinity with pigeons was John Theodore Reinhardt (1816-1882), a curator at The Royal Museum in Copenhagen. Initially, his suggestion failed to bring him much acclaim and for a while it was roundly sneered at. The idea of a connection with the ostriches or the vultures (on account of the massive beak) was, perhaps understandably, more to the taste of nineteenth century comparative anatomists. But just a little later, during 1848, Hugh Strickland and A. G. Melville published their famous book on the dodo, *The Dodo and its Kindred*, and boldly came out on Reinhardt's side, presenting evidence that couldn't easily be dismissed. These two authors had no access to the wealth of skeletal material that has subsequently been discovered, but these later discoveries have only served to prove how right they – and Reinhardt – were.

The evolution from pigeon to dodo may have taken place quite rapidly. Mauritius is by no means an ancient island, the best geological calculations placing it at around eight million years old. On the other hand, the island of Rodrigues – which also supported a dodo-like bird (*Pezophaps solitaria*) – may be younger, it being reckoned that this tiny piece of land emerged from the sea a mere one and a half million years ago. There are good reasons for supposing that this last calculation is based on bogus data, however, so no satisfactory conclusions about the age of dodo lineage can be reached by using it.

The dodo shows a number of what may be termed 'neotenous' characteristics. In other words, the adult bird has many of the features more commonly seen in a juvenile. This is a phenomenon often noted in species that develop in evolutionary backwaters (i.e. islands). The visual differences between a dodo and the familiar pigeon species are immediately apparent and a vast gulf seems to lie between them, yet if one compares a dodo to the squab of a regular pigeon some similarities can quickly be noticed. This idea was developed by Rungwe Kingdon, son of the celebrated African wildlife painter Jonathon Kingdon, while he was producing dodo sculptures at his foundry, Pangolin Editions, near Cirencester, England.

The lack of serious competition allows creatures to conserve energy, and more usefully and economically transform available resources, by maintaining in adulthood a more juvenile seeming state. Unlike most wild things, such creatures do not need to invent strategies to allow them to escape from predators, so they convert this energy saving into other more meaningful (according to their own particular circumstances)

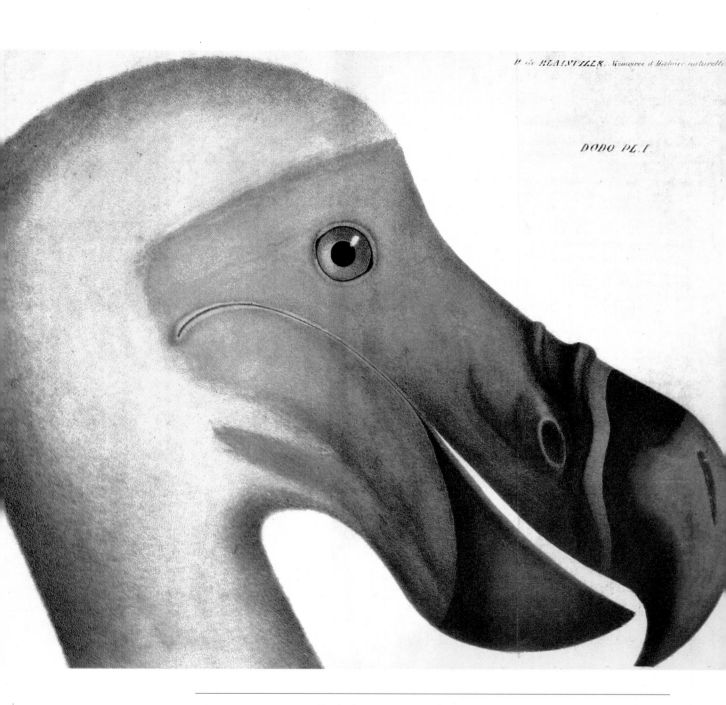

H. de *BLAINVILLE*, *Mémoires d'histoire naturelle*

DODO PL. I

developments. David Quammen who wrote a magnificent book on island biology and extinction and called it *The Song of the Dodo* (1996) summed this idea up perfectly:

As its body had evolved toward greater size, its wings hadn't, and at some point it dispensed with flying. This was a well measured compromise that yielded more advantage than disadvantage. A bird so hefty with such a big head and such a wide gape, could swallow sizeable fruits whole – pounding down big meals and thereby stockpiling nutriment efficiently during the seasons of bounty. Bulked up it could survive through the seasons of scarcity. The smaller species of fruit-eating birds, mincing and tentative by comparison...would have been hard-pressed to compete. On the negative side, flightlessness meant surrendering one means of escape from enemies. But that was an easy sacrifice, since the dodo had evolved in an ecosystem impoverished of predators.

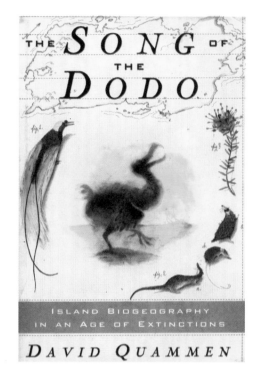

LEFT
The cover of David Quammen's The Song of the Dodo *(1996).*

FACING PAGE
Head of a dodo. Hand-coloured engraving from H. de Blainville's Mémoire sur le Dodo, *in* Nouv. Ann. du Musée d'Hist. Nat. *(1829).*

Presumably, an ancestral stock of *Caloenas*-like birds chanced on the Mascarene islands, colonized at least two of the three, and in the rather unchallenging conditions steadily abandoned the idea of flight. This abandoning of flight ultimately allowed these creatures to bulk up and eventually to grow to enormous size. The process may have taken place over aeons or it may have occurred rather more quickly. We simply have no way of knowing. All that can be said with certainty is that by the time of European arrival on Mauritius this once rather ordinary pigeon-like entity had evolved into one of the world's most curious and striking birds.

The beak had grown way out of ordinary proportion, the head – along with the body – had swollen to comparatively huge size, the legs and feet had become remarkably sturdy, the wings were diminished to a fraction of what might be expected and the tail had virtually vanished or else had assumed a peculiar decorative role.

From the evidence of written descriptions contemporary with the species' final decades it can be deduced that dodos lived in the woods close to the shore. Here, despite their bulk, they could probably move about quite swiftly – within the limits of a heavy bird – in the rocky, wooded terrain that was Mauritius – and they were, perhaps, rather more difficult to catch than might be imagined. Some accounts actually state that they could run fast.

Dodo with guinea pig.
Hand-coloured etching
by George Edwards
from his book Gleanings
of Natural History
(1758–64).

The Dodo

Geo Edwards Sculp. AD. 1757.

294

Andrew Kitchener (1993) has shown from studies on the cantilever strength of the leg bones that the living bird was probably a much more sprightly creature than has sometimes been imagined, with a rather more long-legged appearance and upright stance.

His theoretical work is to some degree backed-up by the earliest Dutch accounts and pictures. A painting by Cornelius Saftleven, now in the Boymans Museum, Rotterdam, also confirms this more sprightly impression even though it shows only the head and neck.

It is really only the well-known paintings of Roelandt Savery (and their derivatives) that have conveyed to the world the image of a grotesquely swollen creature – and all these pictures may well have been produced from crudely stuffed specimens that bore only a passing resemblance to the spirit of the living bird.

Assuming that dodos were rather more agile than is usually supposed, why were they not more able to avoid capture than seems to have been the case? Defensively speaking, their problem may have been one of attitude. With Mauritius holding no natural predators of a size sufficient to trouble them, they would have been quite unused to attack and under ordinary circumstances use of the enormous beak (or, perhaps, merely a threat display made with it) would have been enough to discourage any would-be attacker. Their defensive strategy may, therefore, have been to stand rather than run. Against man this is not usually a successful ploy, of course.

How far into the Mauritian interior their range extended is something that is not known. Presumably, they didn't occupy the entire island. Had this been the case their demise might not have occurred quite so swiftly. One school of thought contends that the species occupied the coastal areas of the dryer west and south of the island and this idea certainly corresponds with those places where the dodo is known to have been seen. Like so much dodo lore, it is complete speculation.

Two icons of extinction: the dodo meets the great auk. Were dodos primarily coastal dwellers? Perhaps. Bromochrome after a painting by John Evans for Country-side *magazine (December, 1910).*

What the birds lived on is also largely a matter of speculation. Certain deductions can be made but there is little hard evidence concerning diet. One account speaks of dodos living on fruit and this certainly seems likely.

The huge beak must have evolved for some purpose but unfortunately we don't know what that purpose was. Probably it tore at large food items as they were held steady by the powerful feet. Perhaps the species lived primarily on fallen fruits, seeds, nuts, bulbs and roots. The suggestion that dodos ate the hard nuts of a tree (*Calvaria major*) known as a tambalacoque, and that this species needed its seeds to pass through the gut of a dodo in order to germinate, has been shown to be false. Dodos may or may not have eaten tambalacoque seeds but these birds played no part in the tree's reproductive cycle. The apparent fact that dodos lived close to the shore – and indeed on small offshore islets that could be reached at low tide – opens up another feeding possibility. Perhaps they sometimes scavenged along the shoreline looking for the cast up products of the sea or maybe they ravaged the carcases of dead giant tortoises. The fact that at least some individuals survived long sea voyages suggests that this was a fairly hardy creature that could adapt (at least for a limited period) to a diet that was none too particular. It is unlikely that any dainty culinary requirements would have been accommodated on board a seventeenth century ship.

In the old texts it is mentioned that dodos swallowed stones, sometimes up to the size of a man's fist. This activity naturally caused considerable wonder to those who observed it. In reality there is nothing too unusual about it. A good number of bird species do this to aid digestion and it is not at all surprising to find that the dodo was one of them.

How the birds conducted their lives is another area shrouded in mystery. It is often stated that dodos were somewhat solitary birds but what evidence there is suggests that this was not actually the case. The records seem to indicate that the birds lived in groups although this might, of course, be an entirely false impression. The idea that these were communal birds is suggested in particular by the account of Volkert Evertszen who encountered a gathering of birds on an island to which he had waded. He says that individuals screamed when caught, causing their fellows to come to their aid. Evertszen's account of dodos surviving on a small offshore island is often held to be the last genuine record of the living bird. If these were indeed the last of the dodos, perhaps there is some significance in the fact that they were living on an island. First, it would indicate that dodos were comparatively unafraid of water (after all they would, like Evertszen, have necessarily had to wade there). Second, perhaps the small stretch of water separating the island from the mainland was enough to inhibit the pigs and the crab-eating macaques that doubtless caused havoc to eggs and young.

The testimony of François Cauche tells of the dodo laying a single white egg on a nest of grass. This may or may not be misleading (certain aspects of Cauche's account are not entirely satisfactory) but, whether it is or not, it seems fairly likely. The fact that any egg would necessarily have been laid on the ground, whether in or out of a nest, couldn't have been helpful to the species' survival chances. The onslaught of mammalian predators may well have left the adults unaffected, but it must have been devastating

The alleged dodo egg (the larger of the two) in the museum at East London, South Africa.

to eggs, chicks and young.

Ralfe Whistler, a well-known dodo enthusiast who lives near Hastings in southern England, has a few fragments of shell with a nineteenth century (and allegedly Mare aux Songes) provenance. These fragments may be from dodo eggs or they may not. Similarly, there is in the museum at East London, South Africa, an egg that is reputed to be a dodo's although most of those who have seen it believe it to be a freak from an ostrich. Unfortunately, tests on the fragments have proved inconclusive and the egg itself has never been exposed to modern technology.

The call was described in one account as being like that of a gosling but other than this description it was never mentioned. Perhaps there is some truth in the idea that the name dodo is simply a phonetic rendering of the song of the dodo. Such a sound would not be entirely unexpected in a pigeon.

How dodos interacted with other Mauritian creatures is another matter that can only be guessed at. It would certainly be interesting to know how they related to the many thousands of giant tortoises that once enjoyed the shelter of the island but are now as lost as the dodos.

It seems unlikely that dodos had any

The skull of a Mauritius giant tortoise, a contemporary of the dodo and, like the bird, destined to become quickly extinct following European arrival.

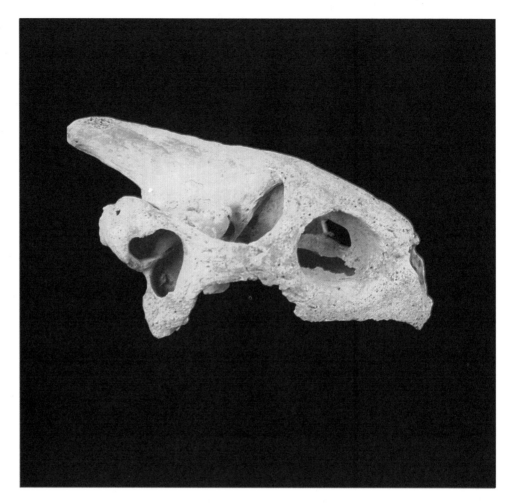

natural enemies until man arrived bringing with him – either accidentally or deliberately – the assortment of deadly predators that he took to many small islands. Rats, cats, dogs, pigs, monkeys all began to roam Mauritius and the dodos, having evolved in their quiet backwater, would have had no more ability (in particular the young) to withstand the depredations of these creatures than they had to withstand the attacks of man himself. There is every reason to suppose that it was the damage caused by introduced mammalian predators, rather than just the persecution by man himself, that resulted in such a speedy extinction. Since dodos were flightless they were obviously completely terrestrial and their size and weight presumably prevented them from roosting even in the lowest tree branches.

Dodo from extinction to icon

A SUMMARY OF DODO STATISTICS

Raphus cucullatus
Linnaeus (1758)

Didus ineptus
Linnaeus (1766)

DESCRIPTION

Beak and head huge; much of face unfeathered contrasting with a hood of feathers on the head; front part of face described in one account as whitish but pictures show it darker; beak perhaps nobbled at some seasons or perhaps in older individuals (otherwise smoother), coloured green and yellow towards the end; wings small, perhaps yellow in colour; body plumage rather sparse with the feathers short and downy, perhaps grey brown in colour; tail feathers curled in peculiar fashion and probably greyish; legs and feet probably yellow with black claws.

Length: approximately 720mm (30in)

Height: approximately 720mm (30in)

Weight: more than 50 pounds (according to Herbert, 1634); modern estimates vary between 10 and 22 kg

Bill: upper mandible 130mm, lower mandible 130mm

Skull: 200mm

Tarsi: 220mm

Call: unknown. One description compares it to that of a gosling.

Food: unknown, probably fruits, berries and seeds.

Reproduction: unknown

Distribution: Mauritius, perhaps the coastal area of the south and west.

The Evidence part 1

PICTURES & WRITINGS

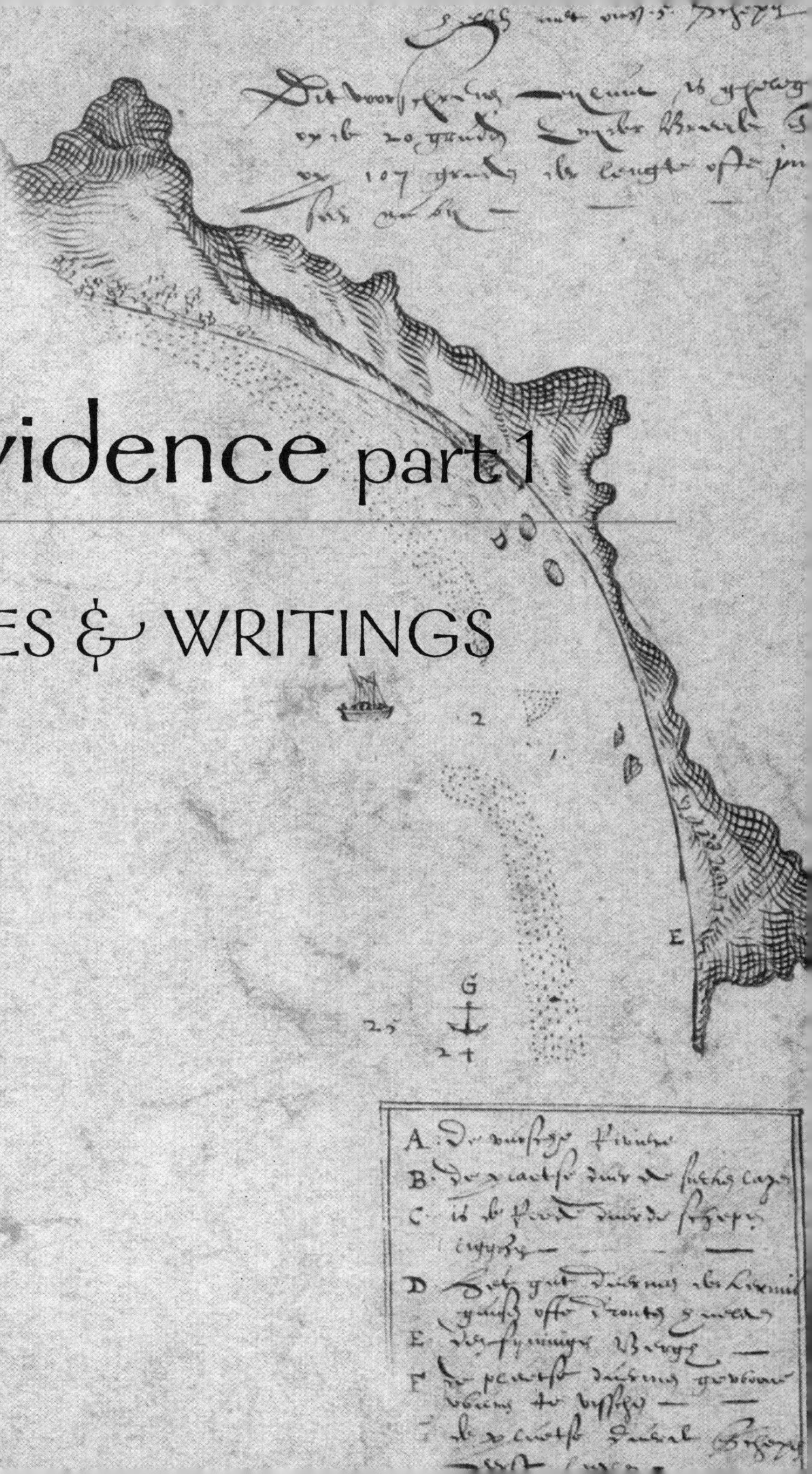

The Evidence part 1:
Pictures & Writings

ABOVE
*Detail of a page from
the journal of the*
Gelderland, *by an
unknown hand.*

PAGE 46
*A dodo.
(Chromolithograph by
F. W. Frohawk from W.
Rothschild's* Extinct
Birds *(1907)).*

The known and certain facts concerning the living dodo could be squeezed into a few paragraphs such is the paucity of the actual evidence. Yet an extraordinarily bulky literature has sprung up from this meagre source material, and page after page of sheer speculation has been written about the species' assumed habits, its possible appearance, the lifestyle and general natural history. Much of this fairly pointless literature is as ponderous as the bird itself. It is often poorly written, badly thought through, wildly eccentric and inaccurate. Generally it consists of one hypothesis erected upon the back of another, most writers on the subject being happy to build elaborate castles in the air with solid walls and ramparts that entirely defy the laws of gravity.

The various theories that have been developed derive from three clearly distinguishable types of evidence. These are: written accounts that date from the time when the species actually existed, paintings and drawings dating from the same period and physical remains (for the most part skeletal).

The problems associated with the first two kinds of primary evidence are quite complex but can themselves be divided into three kinds. First, the pictures and written descriptions that survive from the seventeenth century are comparatively rare. Second, they tend to be rather enigmatic. Third, they contain significant discrepancies; indeed some of them plainly contradict others.

It is upon such contradictions that much unnecessary speculation is based. Rather than offer up realistic evaluations, commentators have latched onto every discrepancy and drawn entirely unsuitable conclusions from them.

What evidence there is needs approaching with a certain degree of care and any reviewer of dodo pictures and writings should beware of over-interpretation. Equally dangerous is a lack of critical sophistication. Almost all of those who have tried to interpret the visual material are guilty of considerable naivety and show a clear lack of knowledge of the aims and intentions of art and artists. Numerous, and serious, problems surround the way in which many of the pictures have been interpreted. Often we have no real idea of the motivation of the

Dodo from extinction to icon

people who produced the images. Were they actually trying to produce a true likeness or was their aim simply decorative? Did their intention fall somewhere between the two? What exactly were these artists working from? A living bird? A crudely stuffed one? Memory?

In many cases the images have little claim to originality. A fair number are simply copies of other artists' works. Sometimes they are copies of copies, sometimes copies of copies of copies.

Then there is the matter of technique. Many early dodo pictures were made by men who were entirely deficient in drawing skills. Others may show more sophistication but still lack an artistic delivery subtle enough to successfully render nuances of detail. Yet successive dodo commentators have taken picture after picture at face value and built elaborate hypotheses on these points of detail.

Similar things can be said about modern interpretation of the contemporary writings. Most seventeenth century descriptions were penned by men with no particular interest in, or knowledge of, birds. Their accounts are, therefore, fleeting and for the most part concerned with the twin matters of edibility and catchability.

A problem that seems never to have been discussed is the very considerable one of terminology. Words can be used to mean many different things and commentators should beware of taking them too literally. What, for instance, might a seventeenth century writer mean by the word 'grey'? He may mean a colour close to black or he may mean dirty white. It may indicate a nondescript shade of brown, a scruffy kind of green or even a lilac or steel blue. Similarly, the word 'fat' can mean a variety of things. Does the writer mean grotesquely swollen or does he simply mean bulky? He may even be referring to the nature of the bird's flesh in terms of its desirability for the table.

The written accounts are, therefore, as tantalizing as the pictures. They may mean this or they may mean that.

The surviving skeletal material is, of course, evidence of a different stamp. However, skeletons only reveal certain things about the creatures they come from and other matters are left entirely unresolved.

So the dodo – despite the apparent wealth of evidence – remains an enigma, a creature of mystery.

Here follows a catalogue of the primary evidence that survives from the period in which man encountered living dodos. Each picture and each piece of written documentation is given a number for convenience.

The Written Reports

These accounts constitute primary evidence concerning the lifestyle, appearance and habits of the dodo. Other reports are either second-hand, fanciful or entirely lacking in any kind of informative content. It is interesting to note that there are precious few that date from after the 1630s and that the content of any later reports is very flimsy. We can assume, therefore, that the dodo was virtually – if not actually – extinct by 1640.

The information contained in the accounts can be quickly summarized. Dodos were found at or near the coast – sometimes on islets to which they could, presumably, wade and, where they occurred, they were (originally) reasonably abundant. There is an implication that they only occurred in certain spots. The dodo area marked on the *Gelderland* map (see p.55) is, for instance, very limited in extent and nowhere else are dodos indicated.

Dodos were upright in stance and the size of swans, with wings that were represented (according to one account) by a few blackish quills, or five or six little yellow feathers (according to another). They sported a peculiar little tail consisting of just a few strangely curled greyish feathers and the head was comparatively huge and hooded. Parts of the flesh were reasonably good to the taste, other parts tough and oily. They swallowed large stones as an aid to digestion, would bite fiercely and had a greedy appetite – apparently for fruit. Their weight was more than fifty pounds and the body was round and fat. Half the head was naked, perhaps some of this area was whitish. From nostril to beak tip the colour was a mixture of light green and pale yellow. The feathering was rather downy and the legs may have been black or perhaps yellow with black nails.

This is more or less the sum of knowledge that can be drawn from the contemporary writings.

Written Report No. 1

————◁◦▷————

Published in *A True Report of the gainefull, prosperous and speedy voyage to Java in the East Indies* (London, 1599) and *Het Tvveede Boeck* (Amsterdam, 1601).

————◁◦▷————

During the last decade of the sixteenth century the Dutch became increasingly determined to develop trade in the East Indies, and towards this end several expeditions were sent out from Holland. The second of these expeditions was comprised of eight ships under the command of Admiral Jacob Corneliszoon van Neck and Vice-Admiral Wybrant van Warwijck; some of these vessels visited Mauritius during the course of their journey. The ships became separated and several (mostly those that didn't actually go to Mauritius) arrived back in Holland long before the others.

A rather rushed and incomplete provisional report was issued but no printed copy of this survives (at least, none is known). However, an English translation of the original Dutch text exists and this was published in London during 1599. In this report can be found the earliest known account of the dodo:

On their left hand was a little island wich they named Heemskirk Island, and the bay it selve they called Warwick Bay...finding in this place great quantity of foules twice as bigge as swans, which they called Walghstocks or Wallowbirdes being very good meat. But finding also abundance of pigeons and popinnayes, they disdained any more to eat of those great foules calling them Wallowbirdes, that is to say lothsome...birdes.

The account reveals very little, apart from the fact that the dodos were at, or close to the coast and that in this place they were abundant. There is some ambiguity concerning the quality of the meat and the size of the birds (twice as large as a swan) is clearly exaggerated.

This last point is resolved, however, in a subsequent Dutch version of the report that was published during 1601 in Amsterdam under the name *Het Tvveede Boeck*. By the time of this publication all the

Warwick Bay – the landing place of Vice-Admiral Wybrant van Warwijck, with Lion Mountain behind. The bay is now more commonly referred to as Mahebourg Bay.

expedition's vessels had returned to Holland so a more complete account (including illustrations) was possible. This new account makes it clear that five ships all under the direct command of Vice-Admiral van Warwijck (not Admiral van Neck, the leader of the expedition, who, at the time, had remained near to Madagascar to provision other vessels) arrived at Mauritius on September 17th 1598. During the next day a good natural harbour was found towards the south eastern corner of the island and the bay in which it was situated was named after the Vice-Admiral, although today it is more commonly known as Mahebourg Bay.

Concerning the dodo, a translation of the new report reads as follows:

There are also other birds there which are as big as our swans, with large heads, and on the head a veil as though they had a small hood on their head; they have no wings but in their place are three or four black quills, and where there should be a tail, there are four or five small curled plumes of a greyish colour. We called these birds Walghvogels, partly because although we stewed them for a very long time, they were very tough to eat, yet the stomach and breast were extremely good, but also we thought the turtle doves had a rather better taste, and we could get many of these.

This clears up the matter of size and perhaps also the ambiguity over the quality of the meat; much of the flesh was tough but stomach and breast were good. Clearly other, smaller, species were more tasty. The strange head is described in a fashion that was to become characteristic and the rudimentary wings and peculiar tail are also mentioned.

In its new state the published report also featured a picture of a dodo in the middle of a landscape depicting many of the activities of the Dutch visitors (*see* picture 1). Two captions are provided for this picture, one of which is fuller than the other, but neither does much more than duplicate information already given:

The dodo in Het Tvveede Boeck.

Caption 1. We have called this bird, which is as big as a swan, Walghvogel, because once having caught the more tasty pigeons and other small birds, we no longer cared for it.

Caption 2. There is a bird that we called the Walghvogel...with a round rump with two or three curled feathers on it. They have no wings but instead have three or four black quills. Our shipmates caught a few...when they landed by sloop. They came back with them with great delight, sharing them with each ship...We cooked this bird but it was so tough that we couldn't cook it through and had to eat it only half-done.

In addition to these remarks in the official publication, some hand-written journals kept by individual ship's captains and other voyagers still exist at the *Algemeen Rijksarchief* in The Hague. One, journal no.51, describes the dodo as having:

The body of an ostrich...a great head and on the head a veil as though it were wearing a hood.

Another, journal no.60, says:

They walked upright on their feet as though they were a human being.

Written Report No. 2

ADMIRAL WOLFERT HARMANSZOON; DATE, SEPTEMBER/OCTOBER 1601.

Manuscript kept at the *Algemeen Rijksarchief*, The Hague.

Three Dutch ships – *Gelderland*, *Zeelandt* and *Utrecht* – along with two smaller ones – *Duifje* and *Wachter* – called at Mauritius on September 30th 1601 and stayed until October 20th. Admiral Wolfert Harmanszoon kept a journal aboard the flagship *Gelderland* (several different hands are evident in the journal, one of which is understood to be Harmanszoon's own) and this two-volume manuscript still exists at the Algemeen Rijksarchief, The Hague.

As far as the dodo is concerned, the most important features of the manuscript are the beautiful illustrations, some of which come from an artistic hand of great sophistication. Written mention of the dodo comes in the caption to these pictures which says:

These birds are caught on the island of Mauritius in large quantities because they are unable to fly. They are good food and often have stones in their stomachs, as big as eggs, sometimes bigger or smaller, and are called 'griffeendt' or 'Kermis goose'.

This caption introduces the idea of the dodo as a bird that uses stones to help in the digestion process, and since this is a fairly common phenomenon in birds there is no reason to doubt it. The expression 'Kermis goose' seems to refer to the day of the Amsterdam Fair – and so has only marginal significance.

The manuscript also contains an illustrative map of the place were the ships anchored together with the remark that **D** marks the spot where one would go to catch dodos. The bay was long thought to be the same one that Warwijck used but Julian Hume, who has researched the matter most carefully on Mauritius (following a hint from a Mauritius-born woman, Claude Kingdon), is certain that it is, in fact, the large bay that extends south from Tamarin Bay on the west coast of the island. It is curious, of course, that the dodos seem to have been present only at one particular spot – and that that spot appears to be a small island!

FACING PAGE
Map from the journal of the Gelderland, showing the bay at the southwest corner of Mauritius. D marks the spot, an island, at which dodos were found.

Dodo from extinction to icon

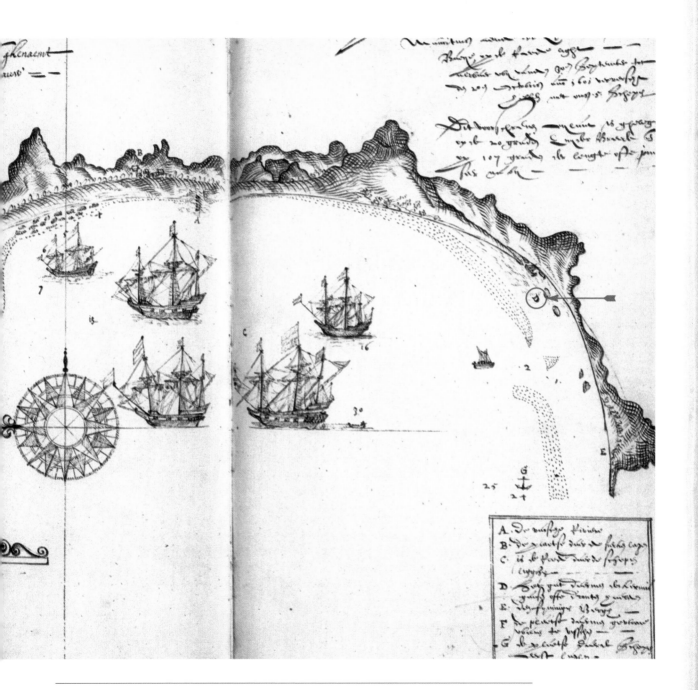

Written Report No. 3

WILLEM VAN WEST-ZANEN; DATE, JULY/AUGUST 1602.

Published in Soeteboom, H. (ed.) (West-Zanen, W. van.)
Derdevoomaemste Zeegetogt na de Oost-Indien (Amsterdam, 1648).

Willem van West-Zanen captained a ship called the *Bruin-Vis* that landed at Mauritius in 1602 on its way back to Holland. For unknown reasons his journal was not published until long afterwards (1648). Van West-Zanen had been to Mauritius on a previous occasion with the fleet of van Neck and Warwijck and some of his remarks derive from that visit:

They caught birds called by some Dod-aars by others Dronte. These were given the name Walghvogel during van Neck's voyage, because even with long stewing they would hardly become tender, but stayed tough and hard with the exception of the breast and stomach which were extremely good…They have large heads with hoods on top and have no tails or wings apart from small winglets on either side and four or five small feathers on the rear a little more elevated than the others. They have beaks and feet and usually a stone as big as a fist in their stomachs.

Later, under the date 4th August, come the following remarks:

The sailors brought 50 birds back to the Bruin-Vis*, among them 24 or 25 Dod-aarsen, so big and heavy that scarcely two were consumed at meal time, and all that were remaining were flung into salt.*

A picture was published along with the text. It shows several parrots being trapped and in the background, perhaps, the killing of a dodo. The image is unclear, however, and no significant information can be taken from it. It is captioned by a poem that can be translated in the following way:

For food the seamen hunt the flesh of feathered fowl,
They tap the palms, and round-rumped dodos they destroy,
The parrot's life they spare that he may peep and howl,
And thus his fellows to imprisonment decoy.

The engraving published in van West-Zanen's book (1648).

Written Report No. 4

CORNELIS MATELIEF; DATE, JANUARY 1606.

————◄◊►————

Published in *Begin ende voortgang vande Vereenigde Neederlandtsche Geoctroyeer de Oost-Indische Compagnie* (Amsterdam, 1646).

————◄◊►————

This report mostly repeats information already published by van Neck and Warwijck, together with the remark that dodos usually had a stone as large as a fist in their stomachs. Elsewhere in his journal Matelief notes that large numbers of rats and monkeys were already on the island.

Written Report No. 5

STEVEN VAN DER HAGEN; DATE, NOVEMBER/DECEMBER 1607.

————◄◊►————

Published in *Begin ende voortgang vande Vereenigde Neederlandtsche Geoctroyeer de Oost-Indische Compagnie* (Amsterdam, 1646).

————◄◊►————

This is another report of rather limited value. It merely mentions that sailors ate dodos at the estuary of the River North-West just southwest of what is now Port Louis.

Written Report No. 6

PIETER WILLEM VERHOEVEN; DATE, 1611.

Published in Verken, Johannes, *Eylffter Schiffahrt ander Teil od Kurtzer Verfolg u. Continuerung der Reyse, so van den Holl. u Seelandern in die Ost Indien mit neun grossen u. vier kleinen Schiffen von 1607 bis in das 1612 Jahr* (Frankfurt, 1613).

There were...birds similar in size to swans, with large heads and a piece of skin over their heads resembling a monk's cowl. Instead of wings they have five or six little yellow feathers, and in place of a tail four or five curly greyish feathers. They are known as Tottersten or Walck birds. They are found...in large numbers, though the Dutch have been catching them and eating them daily, and not only these birds, but many other kinds, such as wild pigeons and parrots, which they beat with sticks and catch, taking care all the while that the Tottersten or Walck birds do not bite them on the arm or leg with their great, thick, curved beaks.

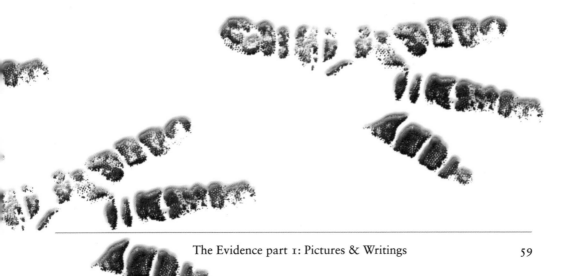

The Evidence part 1: Pictures & Writings

Written Report No. 7

Manuscript letters destroyed by fire during the nineteenth century, before which a copy was made by Alfred Newton.

A fortnight before Sir Thomas Herbert reached Mauritius (see report no.8), a ship from the same squadron as his arrived at the island.

A certain Mr. Emmanuel Altham landed and a few weeks later he despatched to his brother in Essex, England a few presents. These were sent aboard Sir Thomas's ship which by then had reached Mauritius and was sailing on to England. With his gifts, Altham sent a covering letter dated June 18th 1628:

Right wo and lovinge brother,
We were ordered by ye said councell to go to an island called Mauritius, lying in 20d. of south latt., where we arrived ye 28th of May; this island having many goates, hogs and cowes upon it, and very strange fowles, called by ye portingalls Dodo, which for the rareness of the same, the like being not in ye world but here, I have sent you one by Mr. Perce, who did arrive with the ship William at this island ye 10th of June

In the margin to this letter was written:

Of Mr. Perce you shall receive a jarr of ginger for my sister, some beades for my cosins your daughters, and a bird called a Dodo, if it live.

A second letter reads:

You shall receive a jar of India ginger for my sister your wife, as also some beades for my cosins your daughters, and with all a strange fowle which I had at the island Mauritius, called by ye portingalls a Dodo, which for rareness thereof I hope will be welcome to you.
Mauritius ye 18th June 1628.
Your most lovinge brother,
Emmanuel Altham.

The story of these documents is curious but vague. They somehow reached the hands of a Mr. John Wilmot of Tunbridge Wells, Kent who lent them to Alfred Newton, Professor of Zoology at Cambridge University. This loan was to enable Newton to show them before a meeting of the Zoological Society of London and this was done on May 19th, 1874. Unfortunately, the letters themselves were burnt after Wilmot's death but Newton, in typical fashion, had taken a facsimile copy of them while they were in his possession.

This intriguing evidence shows just how interested Europeans were in the idea of sending dodos back home. We don't know, of course, whether or not the dodo made it to England alive.

Also interesting is the fact that Altham seems to be in no doubt that the word dodo is Portuguese in origin.

Written Report No. 8

SIR THOMAS HERBERT; DATE, JUNE 1628

―◄◦►―

Published in Herbert, T. *A Relation of Some Yeares Travaile into Afrique and the Greater Asia* (London, 1634 and later editions).

―◄◦►―

Thomas Herbert was a diplomat and courtier who travelled to Persia with the first English Ambassador to that country. On his return journey he landed on Mauritius. In later years Herbert was to become a close friend and personal attendant to King Charles I and it eventually became his doleful duty to attend the king during the last hours before his execution (January, 1649). When the time came for Charles to step upon the scaffold and face the block, Herbert was so overcome with grief that the king said farewell on the spot and bid his friend come no further.

Herbert's account of the dodo is included in his book *A Relation of Some Yeares Travels into Asia and Afrique* which was first published in 1634, although there were several later editions in which the text was somewhat altered. His matchless and beautiful prose remains by far the most evocative of all descriptions of the dodo:

First here only and in Dygarrois [Rodrigues] *is generated the Dodo, which for shape and rareness may antagonize the Phoenix of Arabia: her body is round and fat, few weigh less than fifty pound. It is reputed more for wonder than for food, greasie stomackes may seeke after them, but to the delicate they are offensive and of no nourishment. Her visage darts forth melancholy, as sensible of Nature's injurie in framing so great a body to be guided with complementall wings, so small and impotent, that they serve only to prove her Bird.*

The halfe of her head is naked, seeming couered with a fine vaile, her bill is crooked downwards, in the midst is the thrill [nostril]*, from which part to the end 'tis of a light green, mixt with pale yellow tincture; her eyes are small and like to Diamonds, round and rowling; her clothing downy feathers, her traine three small plumes, short and inproportionable, her legs suiting to her body, her pounces sharpe, her appetite strong and greedy. Stones and iron are digested, which description will better be concieued in her representation.*

Herbert produced a charmingly primitive illustration to accompany his text but his deficiency in drawing skill limits the value of this picture, although it does perhaps give some indication of the strange appearance of the tail. One curious feature of his account is the mention of dodos on Rodrigues. Clearly, some seventeenth century travellers

ABOVE
Sir Thomas Herbert painted by an unknown hand.

FACING PAGE
King Charles I on Horseback *by A. Van Dyck*

Dodo from extinction to icon

were well aware of the existence of the solitary.

In later editions of Herbert's book his text is slightly altered and although some of the magical character of the prose is lost, there are a few additions to the information given. The edition of 1677, for instance, reads as follows:

Her body is round and flat, which occasions the slow pace...meat it is to some, but better to the eye than stomach, such as only a strong appetite can vanquish; but otherwise, through its oiliness, it cannot choose but quickly cloy and nauseate the stomach, being indeed more pleasurable to look, than feed upon. It is of melancholy visage, as sensible of Nature's injury in framing so massive a body to be directed by complementary wings, such indeed as are unable to hoist her from the ground, serving only to rank her among birds. Her head is variously dressed, or one half is hooded with down of a dark colour, the other half naked and of a white hue, as if lawn were drawn over it; her bill hooks and bends downwards; the thrill or breathing place is in the midst, from which part to the end the colour is of a light green mixed with a pale yellow. Her eyes are round and bright, and instead of feathers she has a most fine down; her traine (like to a China beard) is no more than three or four short feathers. Her legs are thick and black; her talons great; her stomach fiery, so as she can easily digest stones – in that and shape not a little resembling the ostrich.

The fiery stomach Herbert imagines is simply his explanation (common at the time) for the practise of stone swallowing. How else could stones be digested? The whitish face is a new feature, as is the mention of blackish legs. Other evidence suggests that they were yellow with dark nails.

Dodo from extinction to icon

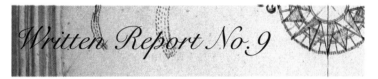

Written Report No. 9

ANONYMOUS; DATE 1631.

Manuscript now mislaid but presumably in the city archives at The Hague.

During 1887 a researcher at the city archives of The Hague, A.J. Servaas van Rooyen, discovered an overlooked, but anonymous, document written by a sailor during 1631. This sailor had travelled to Surat in India and at some point in his journey had called in at Mauritius and seen dodos. His description of the birds is a particularly interesting one:

These Burgemeesters are superb and proud. They displayed themselves to us with stiff and stern faces and wide-open mouths. Jaunty and audacious of gait, they would scarcely move a foot before us. Their war weapon was their mouth, with which they could bite fiercely; their food was fruit; they were not well feathered but abundantly covered with fat. Many of them were brought on board to the delight of us all.

This interesting account introduces some new information about the dodo; most particularly revealing is the fact that the diet was fruit.

Unfortunately, the researcher who discovered the document left no clue as to where the manuscript was stored. Without some indication of its location, there seems little likelihood that it will be found again among the many thousands of documents stored in these particular archives.

Written Report No. 10

Published in Temple, R.C., *The Travels of Peter Mundy* (London, 1914).

Peter Mundy was a widely travelled Englishman who kept a long journal of his exploits which was published nearly three centuries after the events they record. He was an acute and accurate writer and, fortunately, the dodo was a creature that came under his scrutiny. Curiously, he didn't see the birds in Mauritius (although he went there), the which fact seems to indicate that the species was already becoming rare (or at least localised) by the 1630s. It seems to have been a sighting of Mauritius (as his ship sailed passed the island) that inspired Mundy to record his experiences of the dodo. He recalled that he had seen two individuals in Surat, India, an idea that fits in very neatly with the existence of a painting produced for the Mogul Emperor Jahangir whose menagerie was located at Surat. Mundy wrote:

Dodoes, a strange kinde of fowle, twice as bigg as a Goose, that can neither flye nor swymm, being Cloven footed; a wonder how it should come thither [Mauritius], *there being none such in any part of the world yett to be found. I saw two of them in Surat house that were brought from thence* [Mauritius].

Earlier, concerning Mauritius itself, he wrote:

The Dodo. Although wee now Mett with None, yett Divers tymes they are Found here, having seene 2 att Surat broughtt from hence, and as I remember they are as bigge bodied as great Turkeyes, covered with Downe, having little hanging wings like short sleeves, altogether unuseful to Fly withall, or any way with them to helpe themselves. Neither Can they swymme but as other land Fowle Doe on Necessity Forced into the water, beeing Cloven Footed as they are.

FACING PAGE
Mauritius from the sea.

Written Report No. 11

FRANÇOIS CAUCHE; DATE, JULY 1638 (PERHAPS 1640).

Published in Cauche, F., *Relations véritable et curieuses de l'Isle de Madagascar et du Brésil* (Paris, 1651).

François Cauche was a Frenchman whose report on a trip to Mauritius was published some fourteen years after it took place. According to Anthony Cheke (1987), his visit took place in 1640, two years after the date Cauche himself gives (1638). The report contains some interesting features, giving details about eggs and call – but it may not be entirely reliable. What, for instance, do the remarks about the lack of a tongue mean?

On the island of Mauritius I have seen birds that are larger than a swan, with no feathers on their body, which is covered in black down. It has a rounded rump and its rear is adorned with curly feathers as many in number as the bird has years. Instead of wings they have feathers like the latter – black and curly. They have no tongue and the bill is large and slightly hooked at the tip. The birds have long legs which are scaly and only three toes on each foot. The call is like that of a gosling but they are quite unpalatable to eat…They lay one egg, which is quite as large as a penny bun, against which they lay a white stone the size of a chicken's egg. They lay their egg on a nest of grass which they collect and they place the nest in the woods. If one kills the young you find a grey stone in the gizzard. We named them the birds of Nazareth.

Written Report No. 12

SIR HAMON L'ESTRANGE; DATE, AROUND 1638.

Manuscript kept at the British Library (Sloane MSS, 1839, 5, p.9).

This well known account of a bird on show in London is, in fact, the only hard evidence of an individual reaching Europe alive. Doubtless others did (the painting by Cornelius Saftleven, for instance, certainly indicates this) but definitive proof is lacking and many of the paintings cited by ornithologists as evidence of dodos alive and well in Europe were clearly produced from badly stuffed birds. Many quite worthless suggestions concerning the number and variety of dodos that reached Europe have been made. Sir Hamon's report of a dodo seems quite unequivocal, however.

About 1638, as I walked London streets, I saw the picture of a strange looking fowle hung out upon a clothe and myselfe with one or two more in company went in to see it. It was kept in a chamber, and was a great fowle somewhat bigger than the largest Turky cock, and so legged and footed, but stouter and thicker and of a more erect shape, coloured before like the breast of a young cock fesan, and on the back of a dunn or dearc colour. The keeper called it a Dodo, and in the ende of a chimney in the chamber there lay a heape of large pebble stones, whereof hee gave it many in our sight, some as big as nutmegs, and the keeper told us she eats them (conducing to digestion), and though I remember not how far the keeper was questioned therein, yet I am confident that afterwards she cast them all again.

Written Report No. 13

JOHAN NIEUHOFF; DATE, 1657-1658.

Published in Nieuhoff, J., *Gedenkweerdige Braziliaanse Zee en Lantreize* (Amsterdam, 1682).

Although Nieuhoff gives a long description of the dodo in his memoirs (1682), there is no evidence (according to Cheke, 1987) that he ever landed at Mauritius. Cheke believes that the description relates to a bird that Nieuhoff saw in Batavia. This may be so but the notes are clearly derived from earlier accounts and add nothing to what was already recorded. Nieuhoff's account is mentioned here simply for the sake of completeness.

Written Report No. 14

VOLKERT EVERTSZEN (IVERSEN); DATE, FEBRUARY/MAY 1662.

Published in Olearius, Adam, *Orientalische Reisebeschreibung* (Schleswig, 1669).

During February of 1662, four Dutch vessels sank off Mauritius while returning from the East Indies. It seems that no-one survived from the wreckage of three of these but from the fourth, the *Arnhem*, more than 100 people managed to escape in a small boat. This boat was seriously overcrowded and four men were immediately, and callously, thrown overboard on the instructions of the ship's officers. The crew made for Mauritius but during the voyage a further thirteen people were cast into the sea and several others died. Cannibalistic plans were laid to ensure the survival of at least some of those aboard but, fortunately, the island was reached before these were put into effect. More than 80 people

Dodo from extinction to icon

finally struggled ashore. Some of these survivors eventually got back to Europe and four of them, anxious to lay the blame for the atrocities on those responsible, published their stories. One of these was Volkert Evertszen (sometimes referred to as Folquart Iversen), who finally reached home in 1668. He told his story to Adam Olearius, cultural advisor to the Dukes of Schleswig, who published it together with two other reports in 1669.

The wreck of the Arnhem *as imagined by an artist of the time.*

Evertszen maintained that there were no dodos left on mainland Mauritius but that birds of the species could still be found on a small island to which one could wade at certain states of the tide. There has been some discussion as to which island this might have been and there seem to be two main candidates: Ile D'Ambre off the north east coast and Ile aux Benitieres at the opposite end of Mauritius. Few of the offshore islands can be walked to so the range of possibilities is rather limited.

Concerning the dodo itself, Evertszen said:

Among the birds...are dodderse which are larger than geese but unable to fly having only little stumps of wings, but they are fast runners. One party of us would chase them so that they ran towards the other party, who then grabbed them. When we had one tightly gripped around the leg it would cry out and then the others would come to its aid and they could be caught as well.

In the accounts of other survivors of the wreck of the *Arnhem* the dodo is hardly mentioned or else is referred to in words that are clearly taken from earlier published works. Anthony Cheke (1987) who has made a long study of much of the source material is convinced that Evertszen's account represents the last actual sighting of living dodos. He believes that all subsequent reports are either bogus or refer instead to sightings of the Mauritius red rail or hen (*Aphanapteryx bonasia*) to

Dodo from extinction to icon

BELOW AND FACING PAGE
*Two views of the Ile aux
Benitieres. This low
island lies close to the
foot of the mountain
known as Morne
Brabant. Was it the
island on which
Evertszen found dodos?*

which the name of dodo seems to have been transferred. Cheke may well be right but there are some very good reasons (based on the known habits of the rail) to suppose that this record too could relate to *Aphanapteryx*. Other accounts of this rail suggest that it was attracted to the distressing cries of its fellows and it is hard to suppose that one could hold a dodo round the leg without being severely bitten; the beak of the rail, on the other hand, was a fairly innocuous tool. However this may be, it is perhaps a little presumptuous to assume that our knowledge – 350 years or so after the event – of what a seventeenth century mariner did or did not see, is greater than was his own.

GOVERNOR HUGO; DATE, 1663-1674

Manuscript, whereabouts unknown, reported in Pitot, A. *T'Eylandt Mauritius* (Port Louis, 1905).

Although this account is by no means first hand and gives no details whatsoever on the dodo itself, it may be of relevance simply because of its negative content.

Governor Hugo apparently reported that he sent out a party of men to capture runaway slaves and that these men eventually returned with an unfortunate named Simon. Simon had spent eleven years in hiding and claimed that during all this time he had only twice seen dodos.

There are two possibilities. Either the story is entirely bogus or else Simon really did see dodos just twice in eleven years – which implies that the species was at the verge of extinction.

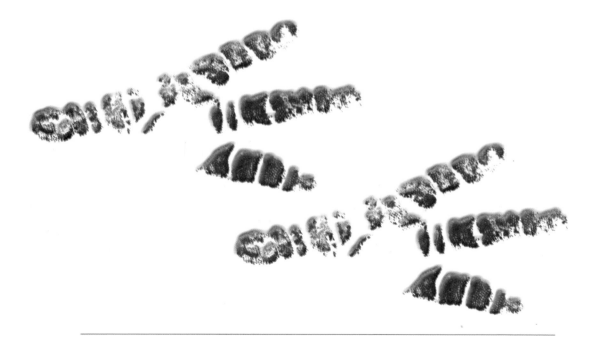

Written Report No. 16

Manuscript kept at The British Museum (Sloane MSS 3668)

Traditionally, this is regarded as the very last mention of the living dodo. Benjamin Harry was chief mate aboard an English ship, *The Berkley Castle*, that reached Mauritius in 1681 and the surviving document that relates to his trip is called, *A coppey of Mr. Benj. Harry's Journall when he was cheif mate of the Shippe Berkley Castle, Capt. Wm. Talbot then Commander, on a voyage to the Coste and Bay, 1679, which voyage they wintered at the Maurrisshes.*

In his list of the 'Producks' of the island Harry mentions:

First of winged and feathered ffowle the less passant, are Dodos whose flesh is very hard.

Whether or not this mention really refers to dodos or whether, as Cheke (1987) imagines, it refers to the Mauritius red rail (*Aphanapteryx bonasia*) will remain a mystery. It may, of course, be simply a reference to a product that the island was previously known for.

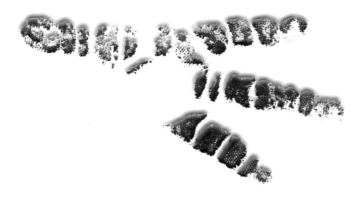

The Pictures

The images featured here are those that might be termed 'original'. In other words those that are judged not to have been derived from previous work. Many other dodo pictures exist but all of these seem to be copied from – or at least inspired by – earlier images.

Where it is not possible to determine from several similar pictures which is the earliest (as in the case of the Savery paintings of 1626) all are discussed together and one is selected, arbitrarily, as the forerunner.

A survey of 'original' dodo paintings may reveal many things. One of these is the fact that these images were all produced before the end of 1638, the last being Cornelius Saftleven's of that year. The many dodo images produced after this date are derivative and are either copies or variants on the earlier works.

What does this mean? Presumably, that living dodos on Mauritius and in Europe were in very short supply after this time and that any new pictures were necessarily produced by copying older ones or by using the same preserved specimens that previous artists had used. As might be expected, this timing of the late 1630s coincides rather neatly with the date at which the written reports get thin on the ground.

The pictures themselves tell us many things about the dodo's appearance. First it was a heavy and somewhat ponderous bird. Although not the grotesquely swollen creature shown in some of the pictures, so many of the paintings and drawings confirm an overall plumpness that the idea of a generously proportioned bird cannot be seriously doubted. Although there is much discrepancy over the matter of the tail, there seems little doubt that this was a most peculiar feature. Some pictures show it longer and more spectacular, others depict it as much shorter; some don't show it at all. The wings were still very much present but far too small to be of use and were coloured yellow. The legs and feet were clearly very sturdy and the claws were powerful. Savery generally coloured them yellow but this may simply have been for artistic effect. On the other hand it may be the natural colour. The overall colour seems to have been greyish although Saftleven clearly shows the neck as brown.

The character of the head is well defined in the drawing in the *Gelderland* journal. Some pictures (Saftleven, d'Hondecoeter) show markings and nobblings on the beak; others don't. Taken in conjunction with some of the writings (which mention green and yellow colouring) we can assume that these markings were certainly present in some individuals. Whether they were a sexual characteristic, seasonal or in some way related to maturity, cannot be judged.

The general quality of the plumage is rather difficult to establish. It seems that the bird was covered in true feathers rather than the more disintegrated hair-like plumage shown in birds that have evolved into a more advanced state of flightlessness (kiwis, ostriches etc). It is interesting to note that the Mauritius red rail or hen (*Aphanapteryx bonasia*) seems to have passed much further down the line of terrestrial adaptation than had the dodo. From this we can assume that the dodo was evolving ever further away from flight and that this evolution was still very much in the process of running its course.

The head of a dodo as imagined by Rungwe Kingdon. Reproduced by kind permission of the artist.

Illustration No. 1

ANONYMOUS ENGRAVING FOR *Het Tvveede Boeck* (AMSTERDAM, 1601).

This picture – which has the distinction of being the earliest known representation of the dodo – shows the Dutch visitors actively engaged in harvesting the products of Mauritius. A dodo is clearly figured in the middle distance and, although crudely drawn, some features are well shown. The curly tail, the small wings, the hooded head, long legs and neck and, most particularly, the upright stance are all revealed. It is, perhaps, significant that the dodo is shown close to the shore.

A picture that is clearly derived from this one was published in the same year in *Variorum Navigationis* by T. and J.J. de Bry (Amsterdam, 1601).

ABOVE
Illustration 1.
*Anonymous engraving
from* Het Tvveede Boeck
(1601).

FACING PAGE
*Engraving from T. and
J.J. de Bry's* Variorum
Navigationis *(1601),
that is clearly derived
from the picture in* Het
Tvveede Boeck.

Illustration No. 2

This painting, attributed to Jacob Hoefnagel, formed part of the collection assembled by the Habsburg Emperor Rudolf II. Most ornithologists who have commented on it believe the model was a living individual but this is almost certainly not the case. Although some of his drawing is a little clumsy, Hoefnagel was well able to render nuances of detail and such details make it clear that here – as with an accompanying picture of a Mauritius red rail (*Aphanapteryx bonasia*) – he was working from a stuffed example. The dried-out, sunken-in features of the face are characteristic of a crudely preserved specimen and so too is the misshapen arrangement of the wing. In the red rail painting Hoefnagel has exactly captured the distortion and twisting of the area around the wing that might be expected in a badly stuffed skin. The general state of the dodo's plumage suggests that this creature had lost feathers either before its death or during the rudimentary preserving process. Certainly, the bird seems to lack a tail. Perhaps it was an immature individual.

Whether or not this dodo arrived alive in Prague (then the Habsburg capital) is not a resolvable question, but by the time its portrait was painted the bird was surely dead.

There is indeed documentary evidence that a stuffed dodo formed part of Rudolf II's collection. An inventory written by Daniel Fröschl between 1607 and 1611 lists as exhibit number 135:

1 Indian stuffed bird, called a walghvogel by the Dutch according to Carolus Clusius. It has a great round body the size of a goose or larger, an ugly large beak, small wings that prevent it from flying and a dirty, off-white colouring.

The only slightly jarring note here is the description of the dirty, off-white colouring, which is hardly a good description of the bird in Hoefnagel's painting.

For incomprehensible reasons, this inventory has been cited as proof (see van Wissen, 1995) that a live dodo reached Prague. It proves nothing of the sort, of course, and the inventory note is simply a record (as is the painting) of a stuffed bird. Whether or not the individual in question even reached Europe alive is an unanswerable question. The evidence simply adds up to the fact that at least one dodo – living or stuffed – was brought back from one of the very first Dutch visits to Mauritius (perhaps even Warwijck's), and that this creature – alive or dead – was taken to Prague where Hoefnagel painted it.

FACING PAGE
llustration 2.
*Dodo by Jacob
Hoefnagel. Oils on
parchment (circa 1602).*

BELOW LEFT
*Mauritius red rail
(Aphanapteryx bonasia)
by Jacob Hoefnagel. Oils
on parchment (circa
1602). Both paintings
are in the National
Library of Austria.*

BELOW
*A well known engraving
by Carolus Clusius
(1606) of a dodo with a
gizzard stone. Clusius
said that his picture was
copied from a rough
sketch in a journal of a
Dutch voyager who had
seen a dodo in the last
year of the sixteenth
century. The picture
shows remarkable
similarities to
Hoefnagel's, however.*

Illustration No.3

In the two-volume manuscript journal of Wolfert Harmanszoon there are several dodo drawings, one of which was produced by an anonymous artist of very considerable technical skill. This picture shows the head of a dodo, which was evidently drawn from a dead bird lying in front of the artist. The drawing was presumably made in Mauritius during the the stay of the ship *Gelderland* in September or October 1601 and it is one of the best pieces of evidence regarding the actual appearance of the dodo's head. Pictures of another extinct bird, the pigeon hollandais (*Alectroenas nitidissima*), are clearly by the same artist and are of the same high quality.

FACING PAGE
Illustration 3.
Drawing of the head of a dead dodo, by an anonymous hand, in the journal of the ship Gelderland. *A secondary illustration is drawn across the fold of the book.*

OVERLEAF
*Two views of the pigeon hollandais (*Alectroenas nitidissima*) in the* Gelderland *journal, by the same anonymous artist who drew the dodo's head. Like the dodo this species is now extinct.*

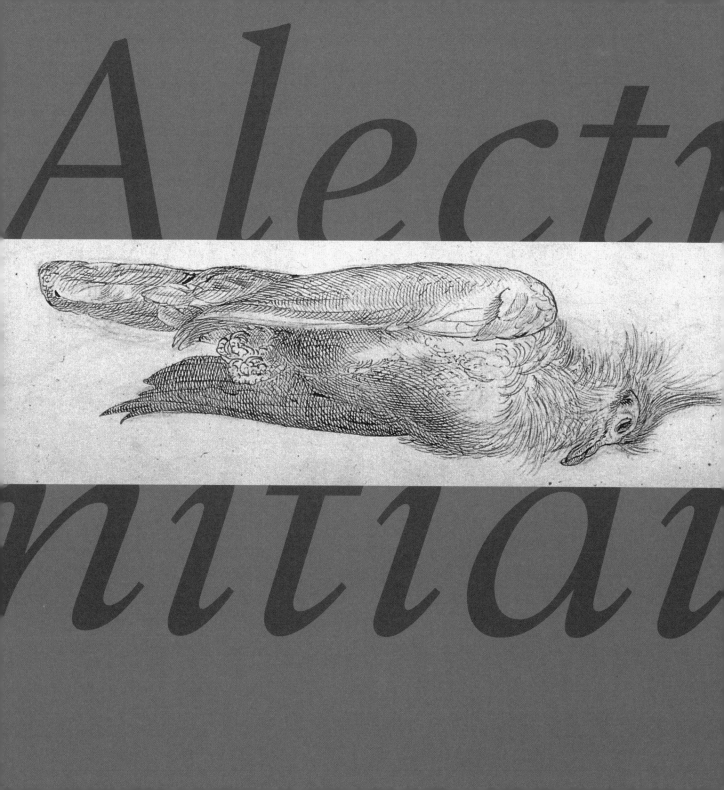

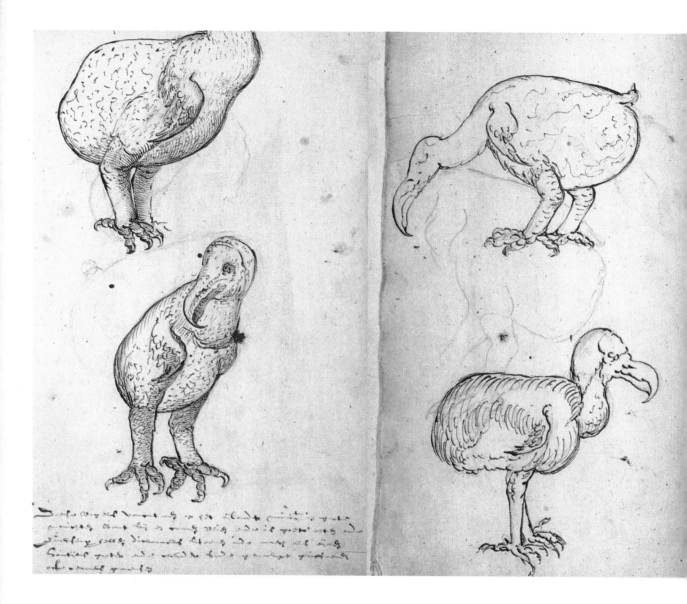

Dodo from extinction to icon

Illustration No. 4

ANONYMOUS FIGURES OF DODOS (1601).
MANUSCRIPT (THE *Gelderland* JOURNAL) KEPT
AT THE ALGEMEEN RIJKSARCHIEF, THE HAGUE.

This is a series of drawings rather than a single image. They are in the same manuscript journal as the previous picture but appear to be drawn by a less sophisticated hand. One is superimposed over the picture of the dead dodo's head (see p.83), which, unless scrutinized carefully, can give a rather misleading impression. The others show dodos viewed from different angles and, although a little crude, perhaps provide a good impression of the bird in life. Julian Hume, the English painter and ornithologist who has made a special study of the dodo, has examined these pictures and discovered that there are several under-drawings and faintly indicated studies in addition to the clearly marked ones. All these images clearly show the sturdiness of the didine leg. Like the picture of the head they were presumably drawn in Mauritius during 1601.

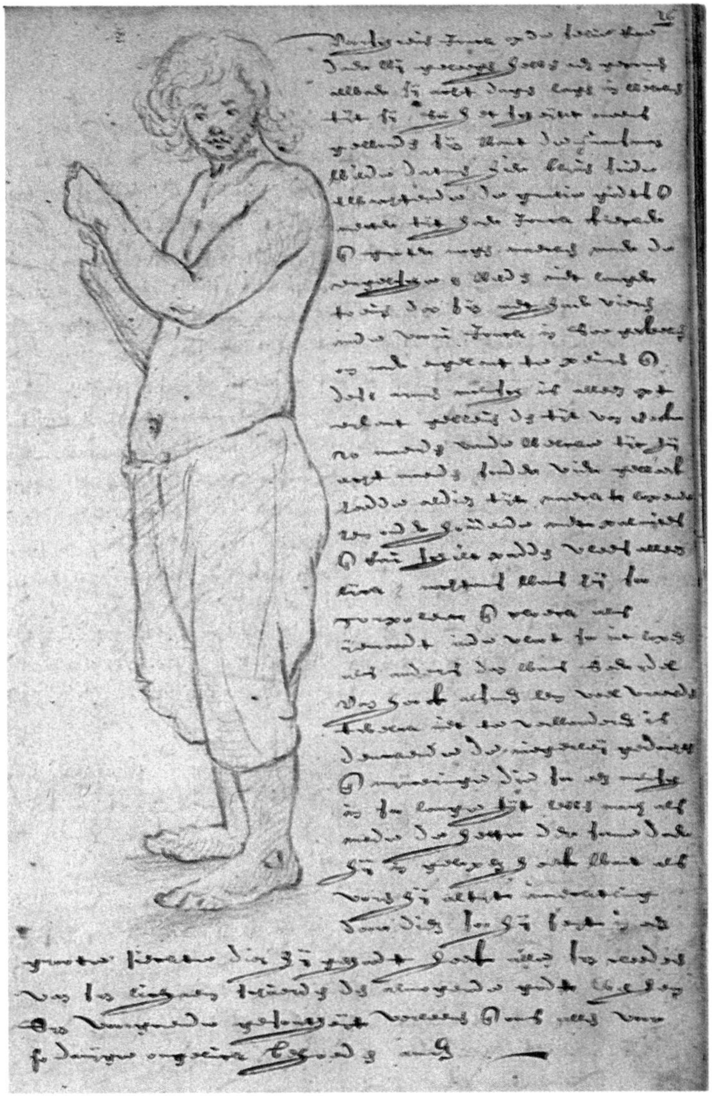

Illustration 4.
FACING PAGE
Two pages from the journal of the Gelderland, by an unknown hand.

RIGHT
A third page shows a sailor from the Dutch expedition.

Dodo from extinction to icon

Illustration
No. 5

JAN BREUGHEL – *Creatures of the Air* (1611)
PRIVATE COLLECTION

There exists in a European private collection a painting by Jan Brueghel, dated 1611, that appears to show a dodo. Only the head and neck are visible just behind two cherub-like figures. Unfortunately, the head is not clear enough for any significant details to be made out and little can meaningfully be said about this picture. The dodo image doesn't seem to be based on any other although a suggestion that it was 'borrowed' from the Hoefnagel picture, illustration no.2 (*see* Ziswiler, 1996), may be correct.

FACING PAGE
Illustration 5.
Creatures of the Air. *Oils on canvas by Jan Breughel. Private collection.*

RIGHT
Detail from Creatures of the Air.

ABOVE
Illustration 6.
Dodo with one horned ram and Mauritius red rail. Engraving by van den Broecke from Begin ende voortgang vande Vereenigde Neederlandische...Oost-Indische Compagnie *(1646).*

LEFT
Dodo, one horned ram and Mauritius rail. *Oils on canvas by Jan van Kessel de Oude (1660). The Prado, Madrid.*

Illustration No. 6

VAN DEN BROEKE – *Dodo with one horned ram and Mauritius red rail* (1617). PUBLISHED IN *Begin ende voortgang vande Vereenigde. Neederl. Geoctr. Oost-Ind. Compagnie* (AMSTERDAM, 1646).

This very distinctive image was probably drawn in Mauritius during van den Broeke's visit during April and May, 1617, especially since the other bird in the picture is clearly the Mauritius red rail or hen (*Aphanapteryx bonasia*). It is possible, however, that it was drawn at Surat which place van den Broecke also visited. Indeed the artist makes it clear that the ram was presented to him in Surat. Unfortunately, there seems to be no mention of dodos in the text of van den Broecke's journal, published in 1646.

Although drawn in a primitive, stylized fashion there seems little doubt that this is a genuine attempt to portray a dodo and it does show some details clearly, most particularly the strange tail and the powerful legs.

The image was obviously used as the basis for an oil painting by Jan van Kessel de Oude which is now in The Prado, Madrid. This particular picture is supposed to date from around 1660 and includes the one-horned goat and what seems to be a rather fanciful interpretation of the red rail.

Illustration No. 7

ANONYMOUS ILLUSTRATION OF A MAURITIAN
SCENE (1619).
PUBLISHED IN J.T. AND J.J. DE BRY'S *India Orientalis* (FRANKFURT, 1619).

Similar in spirit to illustration 1, this picture shows a group of visitors enjoying the spoils of Mauritius: giant tortoises, parrots and dodos. The dodos are too distant to be of value and the figures may simply be copied from cassowaries. It may be significant that they are shown at the coast.

FACING PAGE
Illustration 7.
Engraving from J.T and J.J. de Bry's India Orientalis *(1619).*

Illustration No. 8

USTAD MANSUR – *Birds in the Menagerie of Jahangir* (1625).
INSTITUTE OF ORIENTAL STUDIES, ST PETERSBURG.

The Mogul Emperor Jahangir kept a menagerie at Surat, India. Here, more than one European traveller seems to have seen dodos. A series of paintings of animals and birds was prepared for the Emperor by his court painter Ustad Mansur and one of these shows a dodo. Although the images are a little naive in execution, the other birds in the picture can all be easily identified. Given its limitations, there is no reason to suppose that this dodo image is anything other than a trustworthy representation.

FACING PAGE
Illustration 8.
Birds in the Menagerie of Jahangir *by Ustad Mansur (1625). Institute of Oriental Studies, St. Petersburg.*

Illustration No. 9

ROELANDT SAVERY – *Dodo Study* (1626).
CROCKER ART MUSEUM, SACRAMENTO.

This curious picture, which was copied many times and in various forms, shows two very active dodos in the foreground with a third in the background. It is unlike most of Savery's other pictures both in style and content but the dodo images are certainly connected with those in a painting known as *Landscape with Dodos and Other Birds*. This painting (present whereabouts unknown) shows three dodos, two of which are in attitudes that match the study. Nothing seems to be known of either picture's history; presumably the drawing now in Sacramento is a study for the more finished painting.

Curiously, the study appears to depict birds with webbed feet. Whether this is just an illusion caused by poor – or misleading – drawing skills, or whether it has more significance cannot be determined.

Landscape with Dodos
and Other Birds
*by Roelandt Savery. The
present whereabouts of
this painting are
unknown and the
picture is reproduced
courtesy of Zoo Anvers
and Andrew Kitchener.
Three dodos are shown,
one on the cliff (top,
left), the other two at the
bottom on the right. All
three images seem
derived from other
Savery pictures.*

Dod aers

Dod. aers

FACING PAGE
Illustration 9.
Dodo Study *by Roelandt
Savery? (1626). Crocker
Art Museum,
Sacramento.*

LEFT
*Three later prints
derived from this image.*

The Evidence part 1: Pictures & Writings

Illustration No. 10

ROELANDT SAVERY – *Landscape with Dodo and Condor* (1626).
THE ZOOLOGICAL SOCIETY OF LONDON.

This picture, like the last, depicts a rather active dodo. It is here shown actively scratching its beak. Did Savery see a living bird doing this? We shall never know.

LEFT
Detail from Landscape with Dodo and Condor.

FACING PAGE
Illustration 10. Landscape with Dodo and Condor. *Oils on canvas by Roelandt Savery (1626). Zoological Society of London.*

Illustration No. 11

ROELANDT SAVERY – *George Edwards's Dodo*
(1626).
THE NATURAL HISTORY MUSEUM, LONDON.

Several dodo pictures seem to date from the year 1626 and as all are related works they are necessarily reviewed together. Perhaps the most impressive is the painting by Roelandt Savery now belonging to The Natural History Museum, London. This painting was once the property of the celebrated eighteenth century ornithological writer and painter George Edwards. Edwards presented it to a forerunner

Dodo from extinction to icon

of the present day museum and inscribed a text to commemorate this act across the top of the picture. This rather splendid and bold work has become the model for almost all dodo images – both modern and antique – and represents one of the great icons of extinction. Whether or not it was actually the first of its kind is, however, something of a moot point.

We do not know, for instance, whether it was produced before or after Adrienne van der Venne's well known drawing that apparently dates from the same year. Clearly, the two pictures are related but whether one was copied from the other or whether both were produced using the same rather over-stuffed bird (for a poorly stuffed bird or an over-heated imagination was surely the inspiration for these works) cannot be said. Van der

Manu Adriani Vennÿ Pictoris

FACING PAGE
Illustration 11.
George Edwards's Dodo.
*Oils on canvas by
Roelandt Savery (1626).
The Natural History
Museum, London.*

LEFT
*Dodo by Adrienne van
der Venne (1626).*

Venne's picture is captioned with words that can be translated as, 'This is a faithful portrait of a Walghvogel that I saw in Amsterdam'. These words have been interpreted to mean that the picture was produced using a living bird as the model. They may mean nothing of the sort, of course.

Those who believe that this is an accurate representation of a living bird have argued that the low, bent-legged stance and extreme corpulence is due to an unusual combination of circumstances. Their theory is that a captive bird was grossly overfed on the long voyage back to Europe and that the said creature was kept cramped up in a box that was rather too small for it. Given the fact that creatures taken directly from the wild are not prone to artificial fattening, this elaborate theory is hardly worth commenting on!

It is possible that another Savery painting,

Animals in Paradise (see p.22), dated 1626 was actually the first in this genre of dodo images, a genre that continues unabated even today. This painting is in Berlin at the Gemaldegalerie der Staatliche Museen zu Berlin and a copy of its dodo image was used by Strickland and Melville as the frontispiece for *The Dodo and its Kindred* (1848). Yet another related Savery painting is *Orpheus Charming the Animals*

ABOVE
detail from Orpheus Charming the Animals.

RIGHT
Orpheus Charming the Animals. *Oils on panel by Roelandt Savery (1626). Grafliche Schonborn'sche Galerie, Pommersfelden*

which is in the collection of the Graf von Schonborn Kunstsammlungen, Schloss Weissenstein, Pommersfelden. An additional Savery painting (*Landscape with Dodos and other Birds*, see p.97) exists in private hands and this shows no less than three dodos. It has not proved possible to locate this picture but a poor reproduction indicates that all three images are similar to the better known ones.

Whether or not these pictures were painted at the same time, all are simply variations on a theme. Speculation on whatever provided the original model – living birds, stuffed specimens or even memory – is in vain but it is likely that they were inspired by an overstuffed bird.

A painting by J. Savery, nephew of the more famous Roelandt, exists at the University Zoological Museum, Oxford (see p.12) and bears the date 1651. It shows a gross and spectacular dodo but is clearly just an exaggerated copy of the older Savery's images.

Over the years ornithologists have made much of the Savery paintings, often stating how beautifully and accurately painted they were. The truth is that Savery was by no means a great painter and his work, though often charming, is a little clumsy and crude. To his credit it should also be said that his image of the dodo is a powerful one and the one by which the species is recognized around the world. Almost every single piece of dodo memorabilia – from tea towel to ash tray – is based on it.

BELOW LEFT
Typical dodo ornament of the kind that can be bought all over Mauritius.

BELOW RIGHT
The frontispiece to H. E. Strickland and A. G. Melville's The Dodo and its Kindred *(1848) based on a detail from Roelandt Savery's painting* Animals in Paradise.

GILLES CLAESZOON D'HOENDECOETER –
*Perseus and Andromeda with a Dodo and
Seashells* (1627).
THE DUKE OF NORTHUMBERLAND, ALNWICK
CASTLE.

This rather beautiful painting by Gilles Claeszoon d'Hondecoeter shows a dodo that looks very lifelike. The image is quite unlike any other and gives the impression that the artist had seen a living individual.

Several generations of the d'Hondecoeter family became painters and each specialized in pictures featuring spectacular groups of birds. The most famous is Melchior who was the grandson of Gilles.

LEFT
Detail from Perseus and Andromeda with a Dodo.

FACING PAGE
Illustration 12. Perseus and Andromeda with a Dodo. *Oils on canvas by Gilles Claeszoon d'Hoendecoeter. Alnwick Castle.*

Illustration No. 13

ROELANDT SAVERY – *Landscape with Birds*
(1628).
KUNSTHISTORISCHES MUSEUM, VIENNA.

This painting by Savery shows a dodo in a rather different attitude to any of his other pictures. As is the case with several of his pictures, this one shows a greyish bird with yellow wings, tail and feet and black claws.

FACING PAGE
Illustration 13.
Detail from Landscape with Birds. *Oils on copper by Roelandt Savery (1628).* Kunsthistorisches Museum, Vienna.

Illustration No. 14

THOMAS HERBERT – *A dodo, a hen and a cackato* (1628).
PUBLISHED IN HERBERT, T., *A Relation of some Yeares Travaile into Afrique and the Greater Asia* (1634).

This charming picture is clearly honest in intent but Herbert's rudimentary drawing skills are so woefully inadequate that the image is no more than a curiosity

LEFT
Illustration 14.
A dodo, a hen and a cackatoo. *Engraving from T. Herbert's* A Relation of some Yeares Travaile *(1634).*

FACING PAGE
Illustration 15.
Dodo and Hoopoe. *Watercolour and black chalk by Cornelius Saftleven (1638). Boymans Museum, Rotterdam.*

Illustration No. 15

CORNELIUS SAFTLEVEN – *Dodo and Hoopoe*
(1638).
BOYMANS MUSEUM, ROTTERDAM.

This intriguing picture of the head and neck of a dodo is quite different to any other. It is also the last, in terms of date, to have any real claim to originality. The bird seems so alive and vibrant that it is hard to see the image as anything other than a representation of a living creature.

For unknown reasons most dodo writers either pay this picture no notice at all or else give it rather short shrift. In fact it is one of the very best pictures of the dodo and it is a great shame that Saftleven chose not to show the whole bird.

Curiously, the colouring of the lower neck is very similar to the description given by Sir Hamon L'Estrange:

Like the breast of a young cock fesan

Eccentrically, a few commentators have believed this to be a picture of the alleged white dodo of Réunion. In reality, Saftleven's bird is anything but white and this misconception is entirely typical of the kind of observation that ornithologists make when they try to analyze paintings. Towards the bottom of the picture the painter hasn't bothered to apply any colour other than a light wash. This is simply an artistic device to focus full attention on those parts of the image that he wished to feature, but some have naively believed it to be an indication of white plumage!

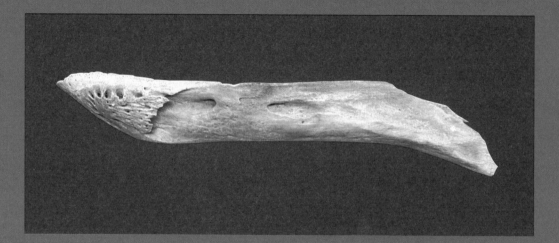

The Evidence part 2

PHYSICAL REMAINS

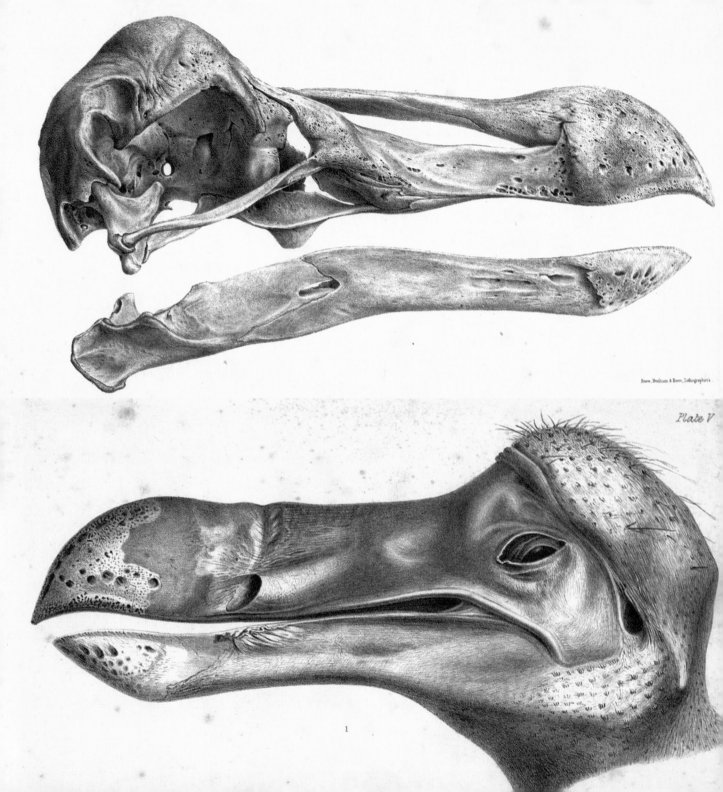

Plate V

Bros. Denham & Bros. Lithographers.

1

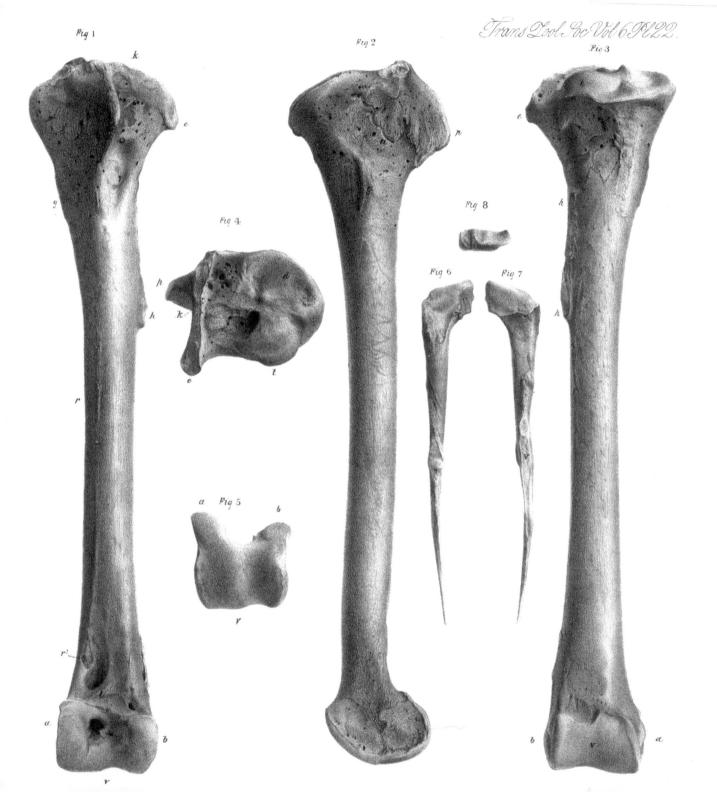

The Evidence part 2: Physical Remains

PAGE 112
*Part of the lower
mandible of a dodo
recovered from the Mare
aux Songes*

PAGE 114
*The Oxford head and
the skull from it
(lithographs in H.E.
Strickland and A.G.
Melville's The Dodo and
its Kindred (1848).
(Shown at 85% actual
size)*

PAGE 115
*dodo leg bones from the
Mare aux Songes.
Lithograph by J. Smit
from R. Owen's Memoir
on the Dodo (1866).
(Shown at 85% actual
size)*

When bones were found during 1865 in a Mauritian swamp known as the Mare aux Songes, the discovery opened up many new possibilities for dodo study. Then, for the first time, more or less complete skeletons became available and these provided a real basis for scientific anatomical research.

The new finds were entirely due to the efforts of a local schoolteacher by the name of George Clark. Before his pioneering work there were just a very few dodo relics in existence: a head and a foot in Oxford, another foot in London, a skull in Copenhagen and another in Prague. These were the sole physical relics of man's encounters with dodos.

Each has a history, although in its way each is enveloped by mystery.

Tradescant's Oxford Dodo

The earliest mention of what was once an entire stuffed bird seems to come in the catalogue to Tradescant's museum, a catalogue that was prepared in 1656. Here the specimen is listed as, 'a dodar from the island of Mauritius'. There is no mention of how Tradescant came by the bird or for how long he had owned it.

John Tradescant was the illustrious gardener to Charles I and this connection with Thomas Herbert has made some imagine that the stuffed bird was brought back from Mauritius by that gentleman. It seems unlikely, however, that Herbert would have brought back a dodo and not mentioned it in his writings. Another idea for the specimen's origin is that it is the very creature that Sir Hamon L'Estrange saw in London about the year 1638. This could, of course, be perfectly true. Equally, it might not be.

By some sleight of hand Tradescant was persuaded to bequeath his collection to Elias Ashmole, the founder of the famous Ashmolean Museum at Oxford.

The dodo stayed in Ashmole's museum for nearly a century. Then, in 1755, the museum Vice-Chancellor and the other trustees made their annual inspection and found the dodo to be wanting in condition and appeal. They ordered it to be destroyed and this order was put into effect on January 8th 1755. The head and a foot were saved from the flames that consumed the rest (the destruction is presumed to have been in the form of a bonfire) and these survive – famously – to this day. Long ago they were transferred to the University Museum of Zoology.

At least two careful dissections have been made of the head, one during the 1840's to reveal the skull and the other at the end of the twentieth century to take DNA samples. The foot has also been dissected.

FACING PAGE AND BELOW
Two views of the remains of the head of the Oxford Dodo (shown at 85% actual size).

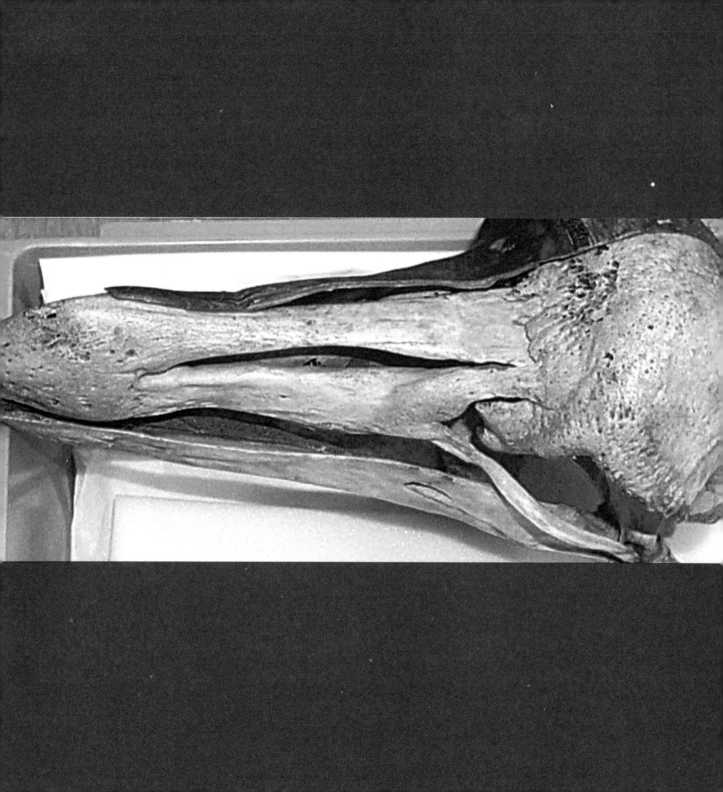

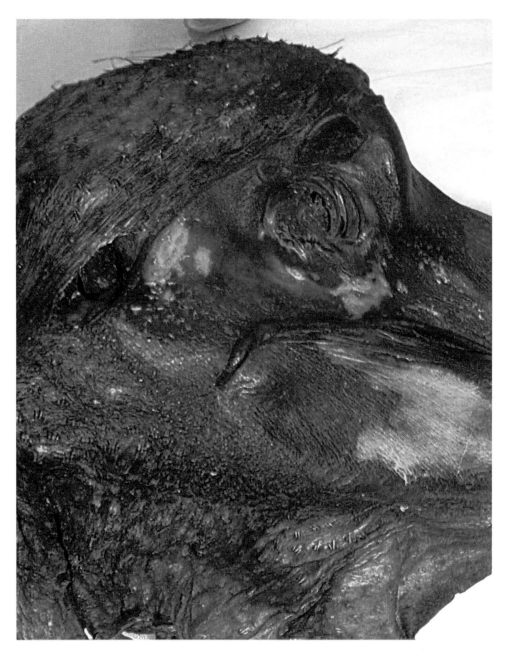

FACING PAGE
*The skull of the Oxford
Dodo.*

LEFT
*Close-up of the Oxford
Dodo.*

The Evidence part 2: Physical Remains   119

The British Museum Foot

A dodo's foot is listed in Hugo's *Catalogue of Many Natural Rarities* (1665) as 'legge of a Dodo'. A few years later (1681), Grew listed the same relic in his *Museum Regalis Societatis*:

The leg here preferved [at the Royal Society] *is covered with a reddish yellow fcale. Not much above four inches long; yet above five in thicknefs, or round about the joints: wherein though it be inferior to that of an Oftrich or Caffoary, yet joined with its fhortnefs, may render it of almoft equal ftrength.*

From the Cabinet of The Royal Society this foot, judged to be considerably larger than that in Oxford and therefore no match for it, was transferred to The British Museum during the eighteenth century. In 1793 Shaw and Nodder figured it in their *Naturalists' Miscellany* (plate 143).

At an undisclosed date it was moved again, this time to what is now known as The Natural History Museum, London. Well within living memory it was safely kept at that institution, but it has now been lost. Whether stolen, accidentally destroyed or simply misfiled is not known.

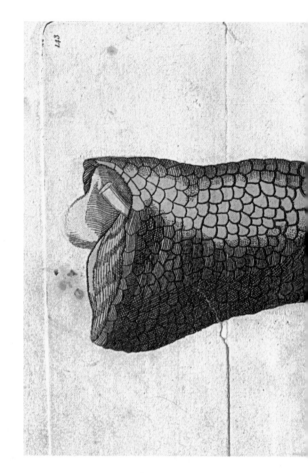

The British Museum dodo foot (actual size). Hand-coloured engraving from G. Shaw and F. Nodder's Naturalist's Miscellany *(1789–1813).*

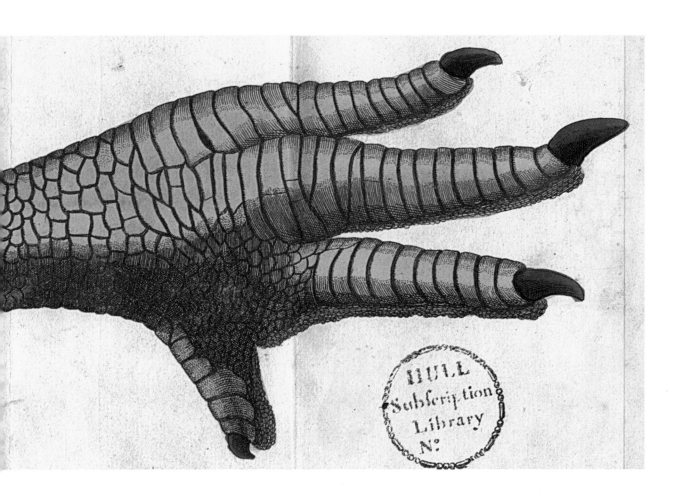

HULL
Subfcription
Library
Nº

Plate VI.

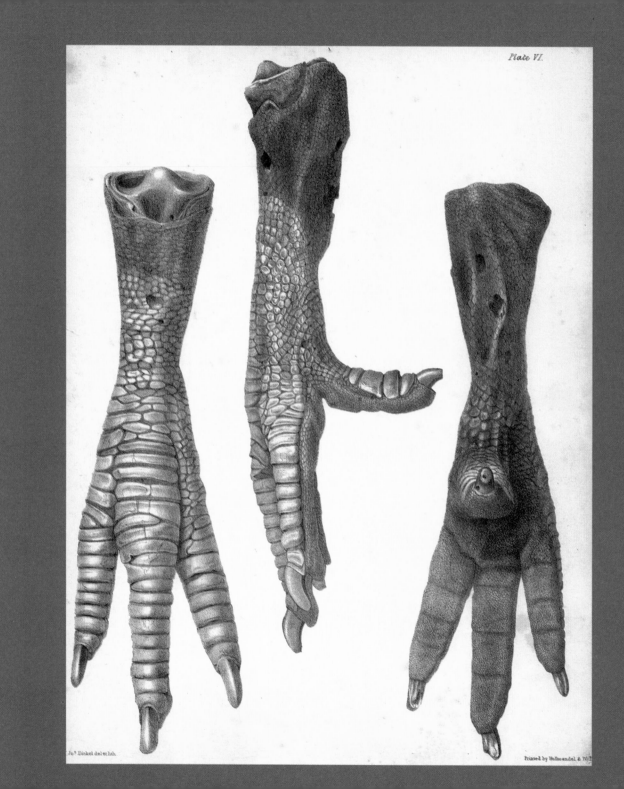

Js.º Dinkel del et lith.

Printed by Hullmandel & W.

The Copenhagen Skull

During 1666 Adam Olearius, curator and cultural director to the Dukes of Schleswig, mentioned in his *Gottorfisches Kunstkammer* that this skull was in the Gottorff Museum at Castle Gottorff. This relic had reached the Ducal seat from the collection of Bernardus Paludanus of Enkhuizen in 1651. It passed out of notice for a period of almost two centuries but at some time during that period the ducal collections were assimilated into the royal Danish collection. Eventually it was located by Professor J. T. Reinhardt, a curator at The Royal Museum, among several cabinets of ancient, unclassified material. Perhaps there is, then, hope that the Natural History Museum's foot will one day re-appear.

It was the finding of this skull that inspired Reinhardt to make his deduction that the dodo was, in fact, a gigantic, flightless pigeon.

The skull is not perfect, having lost part of the bone of the occiput, and it is a little smaller than the skull in the Oxford head.

The Prague Skull

The Narodny Museum, Prague has a rather defective skull that was found, together with some elements of the leg, among the remnants of the old Böhmisches Museum during 1850.

It is not known whether or not this relic has any connection with the stuffed dodo that was painted in Prague by Jacob Hoefnagel during the first decade of the seventeenth century.

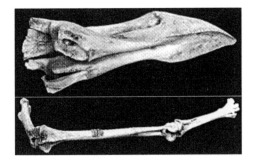

Bones from the Mare aux Songes (and elsewhere)

Apart from the material listed above, almost all dodo bones come from a swamp, four or five acres in extent, close to the southern coast of Mauritius. This swamp, known as the Mare aux Songes, lies close to the International Airport but is situated in the middle of a sugar plantation known as Mon Tresor, Mon Desert.

Here, in 1865, a local schoolteacher, Mr. George Clark, found or, perhaps put more properly, he caused to be found, the vast majority of the dodo bones that now exist in the world's museums.

Clark himself told his story in the Ibis for 1865:

I have been nearly thirty years a resident in Mauritius; and the study of natural history having been the favourite recreation of my life, the hope of finding some remains of the unique and extinct bird that once inhabited this island led me to make many inquiries and researches, alike fruitless. After many years of expectation, I had given up my efforts in

FACING PAGE
Three views of the British Museum foot. Lithograph by J. Dinkel from H.E. Strickland and A.G. Melville's The Dodo and its Kindred *(1848).*

LEFT
Dodo elements in the Narodny Museum, Prague.

LEFT
The marshy nature of the Mare aux Songes.

BELOW
A commemorative stamp issued in 1997 showing George Clark finding dodo bones in the Mare aux Songes.

despair...In September last, some of my scholars... informed me that a number of tortoise bones had been turned up in a marsh...I repaired to this spot called "La Mare aux Songes," and mentioned to Mr. de Bissy, proprietor of the...estate, my hope that, as the bones of one extinct member of the fauna of Mauritius had been found there, those of another and much more interesting one might also turn up.

The estate owner allowed Mr. Clark to use some of his manual labourers to help in the search but since virtually nothing was found on the edges of the marsh, Clark decided to take a different course:

I resolved on sending some men into the centre...where the water was about three feet deep; and there, by feeling in the mud with their naked feet, they met with one entire tibia, a portion of another, and a tarso-metatarsus. I informed Mr. de Bissy of my success...and he kindly gave me the exclusive right to every bone that might be found there...encouraged by success, I employed several hands to search in the manner described; but I met with but few specimens of Dodo-bones till I thought of cutting away a mass of floating herbage nearly two feet in thickness, which covered the deepest

RIGHT AND FACING PAGE
*Dodo skeleton
assembled by the
nineteenth century
comparative anatomist
Richard Owen.
Lithograph by James
Erxleben from the*
Transactions of the
Zoological Society,
London (1871).

Dodo from extinction to icon

findings in several beautifully illustrated works during the 1860s and 70s. Much has recently been made of the fact that early skeletons were positioned wrongly and that the species was much more upright in stance than was in the past supposed. This is unfair on Owen. His reconstruction clearly shows a long-legged bird with an upright stance and a long, almost snake-like neck, entirely in keeping with the opinion of a number of modern authors.

Alfred Newton, the well known ornithologist and author also made dodo studies. In this he was aided by the fact that his brother Edward held the post of Colonial Secretary on Mauritius.

Later, in 1889, more bones were found by a Mr. Théodore Sauzier. Officially commissioned to find them, this gentleman combed the Mare aux Songes and found many dodo remains along with those of other extinct species. Other than this, only a rather mysterious barber by the name of Thirioux seems to have found bones in any quantity, but he was secretive and no-one quite knows where he made his finds. What is known is the fact that he spent thirty years poking around in caves and in places where there had been soil erosion. At the end of this time it seems that he had assembled more than one complete dodo skeleton together with those of other extinct Mauritian vertebrates.

Dodo bones from the Mare aux Songes.

part of the marsh. In the mud under this, I was rewarded by finding the bones of many Dodos.

Clark's finds enabled the nineteenth century comparative anatomist Sir Richard Owen (more famous for his work on dinosaurs and moas) to make a serious study of the bird's skeleton and he published his

A LIST OF MUSEUMS WITH SIGNIFICANT HOLDINGS OF DODO MATERIAL

Museum	Location	Material
Geological and Mineralogical Museum, Delft	Amsterdam/Delft	Almost complete skeleton on loan to The Zoological Museum of the University of Amsterdam
Humboldt University Zoological Museum	Berlin	Bones
Booth Museum of Natural History	Brighton	Partial skeleton and many bones
Royal Belgian Institute of Natural Sciences	Brussels	Partial skeleton
U.K. Zoological Museum of the University	Cambridge	Almost complete skeleton and many loose bones
Museum of Comparative Zoology	Cambridge, Mass.	Two partial skeletons
City Museum	Cardiff	Partial skeleton
National Museum of Natural History	Dublin	Partial skeleton
Durban Museum	Durban	Almost complete skeleton
National Museums of Scotland	Edinburgh	Partial skeleton
Senckenberg Museum	Frankfurt	Almost complete skeleton
Zoological Museum	Copenhagen	Skull
Durrell Wildlife Conservation Trust	Jersey	Partial skeleton on loan from the Mauritius Institute
Natural History Museum	La Rochelle	Almost complete skeleton
National Museum of Natural History	Leiden	Bones
The Natural History Museum	London	Two almost complete skeletons, one of which is kept at Tring, Herts; many bones. Foot, lost
University College	London	Almost complete skeleton
Museum of Natural History	Lyons	Almost complete skeleton
American Museum of Natural History	New York	Almost complete skeleton; many bones
University Museum of Zoology	Oxford	Head and right foot; partial skeleton
National Museum of Natural History	Paris	Almost complete skeleton; many bones
Mauritius Institute	Port Louis (Mauritius)	Two almost complete skeletons; many bones
Narodny Museum	Prague	Partial skull and leg bones
National Museum of Natural History	Washington	Almost complete skeleton
Natural History Museum	Vienna	Partial skeleton
University of Zanzibar?	Zanzibar	Partial skeleton

After Extinction

THE DODO & MAN

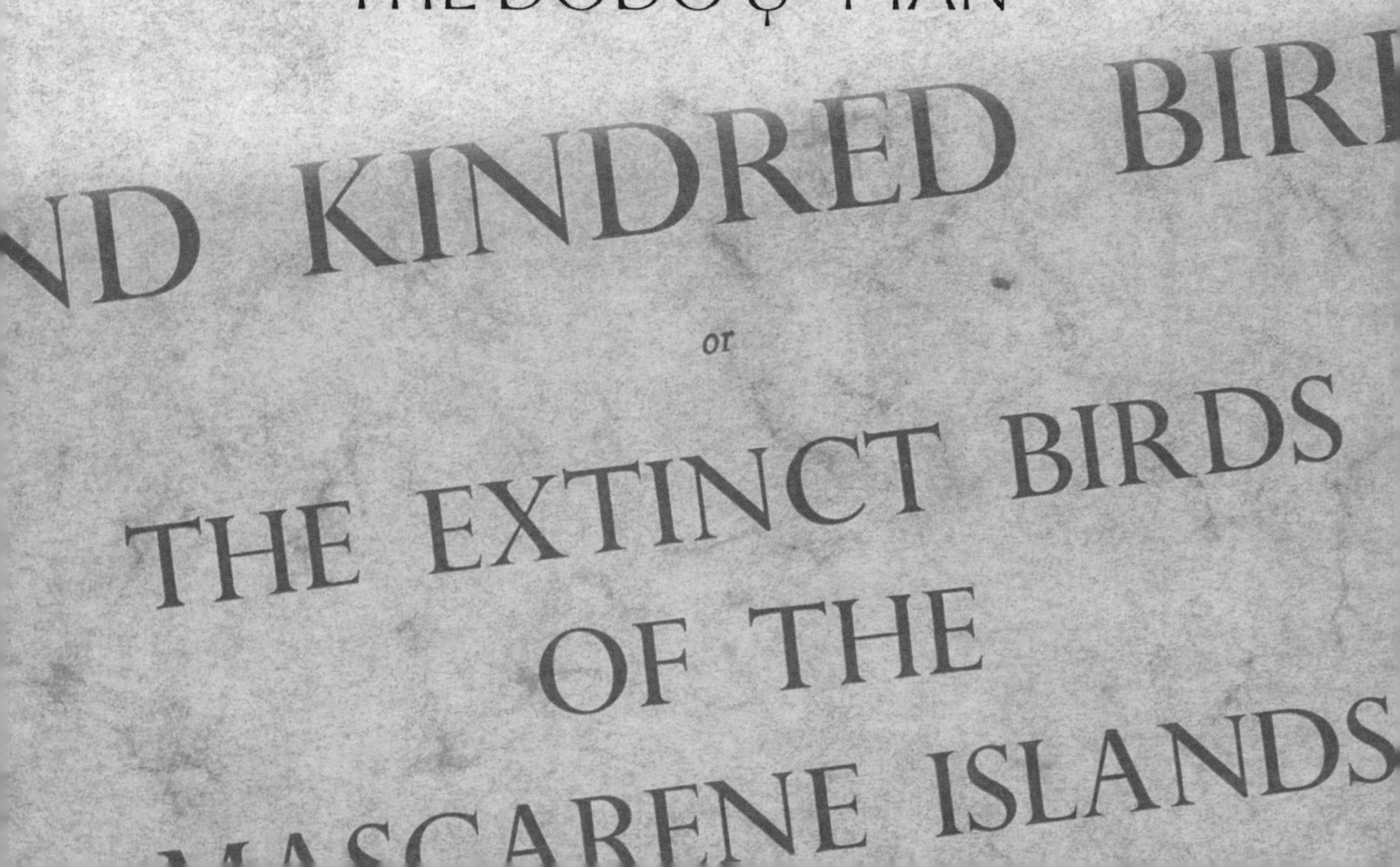

ND KINDRED BIRI

or

THE EXTINCT BIRDS

OF THE

MASCARENE ISLANDS

After Extinction: the Dodo & Man

This Pleasing Bird, I grieve to own
Is now Extinct. His Soul has Flown
To Parts Unknown, beyond the Styx
To join the Archoeopteryx.
What Strange, Inexplicable Whim
Of Fate, was it to banish him?
When Every Day the numbers swell
Of creatures we could spare so well:
Insects that Bite, and snakes that sting,
And many another Noxious Thing.
All these, my Child, had I my Say,
Should be Extinct this very Day.
Then would I send a Special Train
To bring the Do-do back again.

OLIVER HERFORD (1901)

O ur knowledge of the dodo as an actual, living, breathing bird is limited. Very limited. Yet in popular culture it is one of the best known of creatures, and ranks with tigers, penguins, elephants and dinosaurs as an animal that most children will recognize. It is the ultimate symbol of what can go wrong when man and nature come together.

Strangely, this promotion to animal stardom is a phenomenon that began long after the bird itself was gone. Although a few individuals were doubtless brought back from Mauritius to Europe in the early 1600s – and these birds seem to have acquired some celebrity – the species was soon forgotten and only antiquaries and avid natural historians remembered it. Then came a time when even the very fact of its one-time existence was questioned and the learned (or at least some of them) supposed that the various seventeenth century paintings that depict it were fanciful works of the imagination.

Then, in the early nineteenth century, the species seems to have enjoyed something of a minor renaissance. Certainly, it was widely discussed in zoological circles and naturalists began to realize that a few – a very few – relics of it survived. There was a head and foot in Oxford, another foot in London, a skull in Copenhagen, another in Prague. And there were the paintings, some of them by very sophisticated artistic hands.

There was some debate over just what kind of bird this might have been. An ostrich

PAGE 130
A dodo biscuit barrel (circa 1980). Photo by Rob Chinery.

ABOVE
A typical late eighteenth century engraving of a dodo.

FACING PAGE
A collection of small souvenir metal dodo ornaments (circa 1999). Photos by Rob Chinery.

type, some said. Others thought vulture was more likely. Still others argued for gallinaceous birds. Then, in 1841, John Theodore Reinhardt (1816-82), a curator at The Royal Museum, Copenhagen, hit on the word pigeon. So laughable did this suggestion seem that most commentators dismissed it out of hand. There the matter rested until the year 1848 when H.E. Strickland and A.G. Melville published a wonderful (and now rare and valuable) book called *The Dodo and its Kindred*. Much to the surprise of the scientific community, Strickland and Melville threw their weight solidly behind the pigeon hypothesis, providing various irrefutable proofs, and the reputation of Professor Reinhardt was vindicated. The dodo was indeed a giant, flightless bird of the pigeon kind.

The great naturalists of the day, men like Richard Owen, Alfred Newton, John Wolley, began to study dodos in earnest. Their work,

and the pigeon discovery, may have galvanized the zoological community but it was probably of minimal interest to the world at large.

One single event caused the general public to take notice of the dodo, and the bird itself to enter the ranks of universal celebrity. This was the publication in 1865 of Lewis Carroll's (or Charles Dodgson, as he was really named) *Alice's Adventures in Wonderland*. This publication coincided (almost) with the production of one of Richard Owen's well-known monographs on the skeleton of the dodo and, indeed, with the discovery of dodo bones in the Mare aux Songes.

Carroll was, apparently, in the habit of taking walks with the little girl who was to be immortalized as Alice, and one of their favourite excursions was to go to see the dodo remains in the museum at Oxford. Concerning the dodo, he wrote in his typical style:

The real Alice, inspiration for Alice's Adventures in Wonderland.

This question the Dodo could not answer without a great deal of thought, and it sat for a long time with one finger pressed upon its forehead (the position in which you usually see Shakespeare, in the pictures of him), while the rest waited in silence. At last the Dodo said, "Everybody has won, and all must have prizes."
"But who is to give the prizes?" quite a chorus of voices asked.
"Why, she, of course," said the Dodo, pointing to Alice with one finger; and the whole party at once crowded round her, calling out in a confused way, "Prizes! Prizes!"

As is evident from the above, the scene in which the dodo figures is a relatively uninspiring one, and it wasn't so much the

Two illustrations for
Alice's Adventures in
Wonderland.
ABOVE
by Sir John Tenniel
(1865).
OVERLEAF
by Angel Dominguez
(1996).

ABOVE RIGHT
A memorial window in a church at Daresbury where Lewis Carroll spent his childhood.

FACING PAGE
An illustration accompanying Oliver Herford's poem (see p.133) from his book More Animals *(1901).*

inclusion of a dodo in the narrative that made the difference in public awareness. It was the illustrative power of Sir John Tenniel, who produced the pictures for Carroll's book. His dodo, leaning on a cane, with the bird itself based firmly on the seventeenth century pictures of Roelandt Savery, made for an unforgettable image.

The enormous popularity of *Alice's Adventures in Wonderland* brought the dodo to a very wide audience indeed. The dodo, like the book, was suddenly in vogue and – again just like the book – it has never since been out of it.

Dodos began to feature in all kinds of children's stories. Dodo poems are a fairly common phenomenon and the one that heads

this chapter is a fairly typical, albeit rather superior, example. It was written by one Oliver Herford and appears, along with a picture, in an American book of children's poems entitled *More Animals* that was published in New York during 1901.

A somewhat less interesting poem was written by the far more famous Hilaire Belloc:

The Dodo used to walk around
And take the sun and air.
The sun yet warms his native ground –
The Dodo is not there!

The voice which used to squawk and squeak
Is now forever dumb –
Yet you may see his bones and beak
All in the Mu-se-um.

Articles about dodos commonly occurred in the popular newspapers, magazines and journals (they still do!) and the word became a fashionable nickname for girls. Even today

Fresh Whole Salmon
£1.47
per lb

RIGHT
Derek the Dodo. *A cartoon character invented for an advertising campaign run by the British supermarket chain Tesco. This campaign featured the logo, 'buy now, they won't be around forever'.*

ABOVE
Derek the Dodo. *Stuffed toys that were available to promote the campaign. Photo by Rob Chinery.*

there are a surprisingly large number of female dodos.

Being one of the great icons of the animal kingdom, the dodo's image can crop up in the most unexpected places – on a tea-towel, a box of matches, a coffee mug or a set of stamps. Surprisingly perhaps, because of the negative image of an extinct species, dodos even turn up in advertising campaigns. A recent one in Great Britain that ran on television and in the newspapers used a cartoon dodo named Derek to drum up business for the supermarket chain Tesco.

Featuring Derek the Dodo in all kinds of predicaments, the caption (revealing the concept around which the whole campaign was based) read, 'buy now, they won't be around forever'.

Almost every single piece of dodo marketing or merchandising is fronted by an image that is directly descended from the famous paintings of Roelandt Savery. If Sir John Tenniel started the trend, many others have been there to continue it. Painters, sculptors and designers simply borrow and re-borrow from him over and over again.

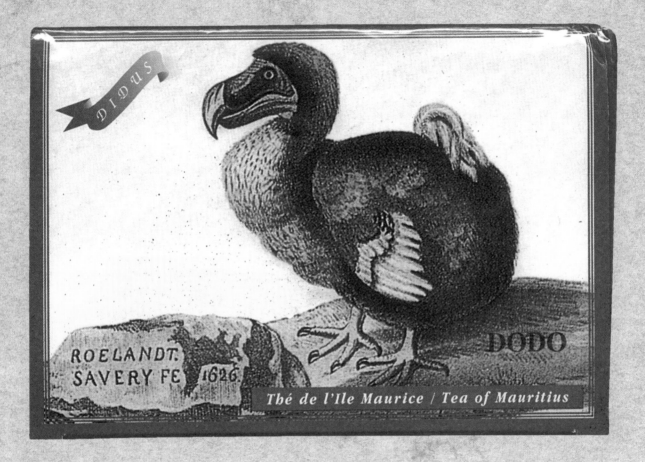

DIDUS

DODO

Thé de l'Ile Maurice / Tea of Mauritius

ROELANDT. SAVERY FE 1626.

A packet of dodo tea, the kind of tourist product available all over Mauritius, showing the illustrative influence of Roelandt Savery.

FAR RIGHT
*Benjii Moss and his
chewing gum dodo.*

RIGHT
*a logo designed for the
sides of trucks owned by
the Jersey wildlife
Preservation Trust.*

The image occurs as the emblem for The Jersey Wildlife Preservation Trust, an organization with a world-wide reputation for its dedication to the cause of saving endangered species. This is, of course, an understandable connection. The connection with a work by Benjii Moss, an artist from Glasgow, also makes coherent sense. He came up with the idea of making a dodo out of used chewing gum. Mr. Moss was a heavy smoker who turned to the gum to help him give up his habit. Whenever he finished with a piece he added it to his sculpture. The chewing gum, he believed, was helping to prevent him from becoming as extinct as a dodo!

Other uses of the dodo image seem more obscure. Some people have headed notepaper featuring dodos. There is something called a 'dodo pad' – a product rather like a diary – that is issued every year.

Dodos regularly feature in cartoon spreads

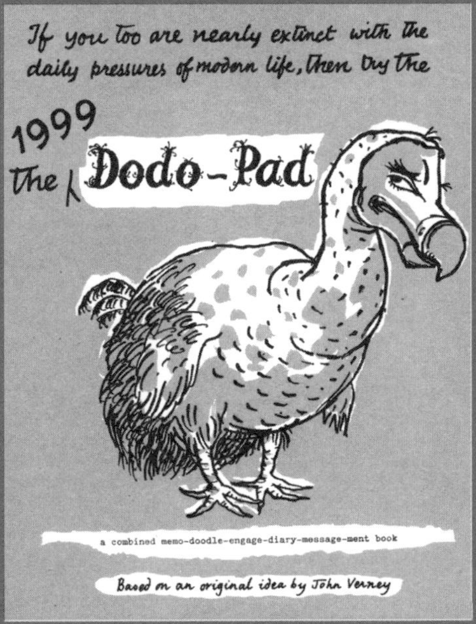

If you too are nearly extinct with the daily pressures of modern life, then try the

1999

The Dodo-Pad

a combined memo-doodle-engage-diary-message-ment book

Based on an original idea by John Verney

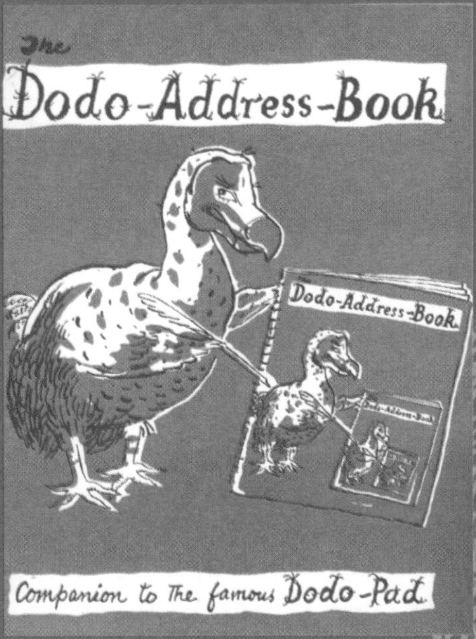

The Dodo-Address-Book

Companion to the famous Dodo-Pad

Dodo pad and address book. This product is issued every year and, clearly, enjoys commercial success.

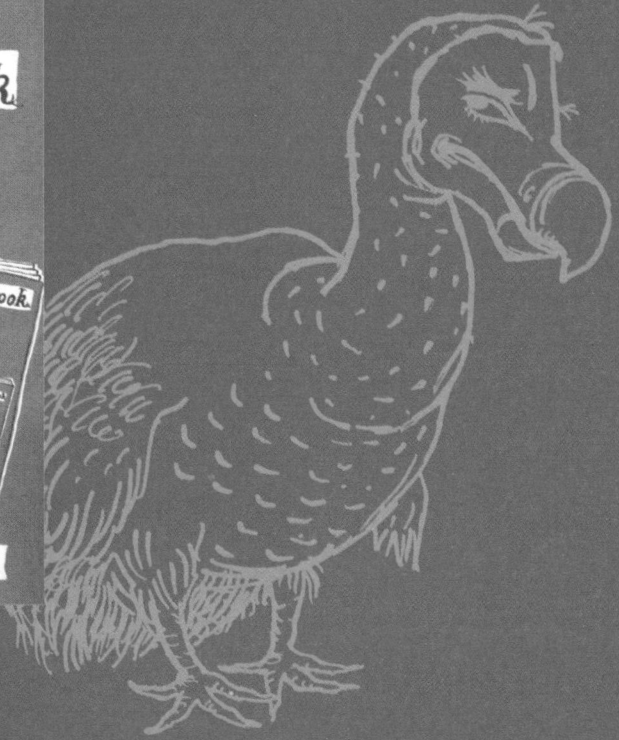

Dodo headed notepaper. Curiously, these motifs have been used by two residents of Hastings, East Sussex, England, 100 years apart.

RIGHT
The notepaper of Ralfe Whistler, dodo collector.

FAR RIGHT
The notepaper of Thomas Parkin, author of a celebrated paper on another extinct bird, the great auk, which was written during 1911.

Corporation Museum, Hastings.
22nd October, 1907.

RIGHT
Ralfe Whistler, doyen of dodo collectors, in his garden near Hastings, East Sussex, England.

and they have done so for well over a century. There are special dodo gardens with statuettes or topiary hedges cut into dodo shapes. One famous 'dodo garden' is at Mount Stewart House, Newtonards, County Down, Northern Ireland where it was created by the Marchioness of Londonderry.

Then there are the dodo collectors. Stuffed toys, ceramic ornaments, pictures, cartoons, books, models - all, and much else, falls within their remit. Some collectors are more extreme than others and these people fill entire houses with memorabilia; some even name their house after the bird. There are several 'dodo houses'.

To acquire a comprehensive collection of books with the word dodo in the title could easily become a lifetime's work. Titles like *Such Darling Dodos*, *Dodo's Schooldays*, *The Dodo Garden* or even just plain, simple *Dodo* abound; there are hundreds of them. Most have absolutely nothing to do with the bird. Then there are children's books. Every year sees the publication of books with titles like, *I Wonder Why the Dodo is Extinct?*, *Dodo Doodle's Homework*, *In Dodoland* or *I, the Dodo*. Such titles occur in many languages: *La Légende du Dodo*, *Heureux Dodo*, *Der Dodo, Der Dodo*.

BELOW
*A dodo bookshelf.
Photo by Rob Chinery.*

Four dodo books written for children. Many such books are produced every year.

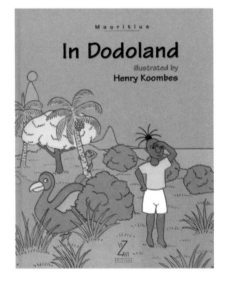

An assembly of dodo memorabilia. Photo by Rob Chinery.

Genuine dodo literature – by which is meant ornithological writing rather than literary – is characterized by its remarkably poor scholarship. Perhaps because dodo study is necessarily spread over many disciplines – artistic, historical, archival, ornithological, osteological etc. – there has been little quality control. Ornithologists have made ludicrous assumptions when looking at paintings, historians have shown a complete lack of knowledge of birds and there has been a widespread and very general interdisciplinary confusion. Added to this is the difficulty of language. Many of the early reports are in old Dutch and they are in inaccessible places or occur only in excessively rare books. Despite the fact that there is so little actual primary source material, the dodo has probably been considered as much as any bird, but there cannot be another species which has attracted so much unfounded gossip and rumour.

Even the scientific name for the species, *Raphus cucullatus*, has caused confusion. *Cucullatus* was coined by Linnaeus in 1758 and his name was joined to *Raphus*, given by Brisson. The Linnaean part of the name, *cucullatus*, is perfectly appropriate: it is a late Latin word for 'hooded'. Yet *Raphus* is

THE DODO
AND KINDRED BIRDS

or

THE EXTINCT BIRDS
OF THE
MASCARENE ISLANDS

VICTORIORNIS

By

MASAUJI
HACHISUKA

Ph.D., Sc.D.

DODO-STUDIËN

Naar aanleiding van de vondst van een gevelsteen
met Dodo-beeld van 1561 te Vere

DOOR

Dr. A. C. OUDEMANS.

Verhandelingen der Koninklijke Akademie van Wetenschappen te Amsterdam.
(TWEEDE SECTIE).
DEEL XIX. N°. 4.
Met 15 Platen.

AMSTERDAM,
JOHANNES MÜLLER.
Juni 1917.

The covers of two rare, but eccentric and unreliable books – Hachisuka's The Dodo and Kindred Birds *(1953) and Oudemans's* Dodo-Studien *(1917).*

THE LAST OF THE QUAGGAS JOINS THE GREAT EXTINCT

"I feel really confident about our future now"

misleading, being based on a Greek word that relates to the avian family of bustards. A rather better name was given by Linnaeus himself some nine years after the first. This is *Didus ineptus*, which speaks for itself. Unfortunately, the rules of nomenclatural priority negate this later name.

Unlike many later books, the very first one devoted to the dodo was a model of scientific rigour and after the passing of more than 150 years it remains by far the best work on the subject. This is *The Dodo and its Kindred* (1848) by H.E. Strickland and A.G. Melville. There are two later books, in particular, that contain so many errors, misunderstandings, totally unsubstantiated ideas and plain sloppy scholarship that they are virtually worthless despite the fact that both authors had collected together a wealth of material. These are *The Dodo and Kindred Birds* (1953), with a title suspiciously like that of the Strickland and Melville book, and *Dodo-Studien* (1917). The first was written by a Japanese enthusiast Masauji Hachisuka who, in fairness, must have encountered serious difficulty over

language. Despite the mass of material he assembled, he was, unfortunately, unable to direct it in a focused way. The second book, *Dodo-Studien*, was written by a Dutch professor and expert on sea serpents, A.C. Oudemans, whose mind was obviously attracted to the marvellous. His ideas and conclusions are, for the most part, suspect

The dodo as an icon of extinction – three cartoons that clearly show a universal understanding of the meaning of the dodo. The image above right was published in the Evening Standard *after the British general election of 2001 and shows the assumed plight of the British Conservative Party. The sources of the other two images are unknown.*

FACING PAGE
The covers of two rare but eccentric and unreliable books – Hachisuka's The Dodo and Kindred Birds *(1953) and Oudemans'* Dodo-Studien *(1917).*

A gallery of dodo men

TOP ROW FROM THE LEFT

Antoon Cornelius Oudemans, author of Dodo-Studien; *Sir Richard Owen, author of* Memoir on the Dodo, *with his granddaughter; Lewis Carroll, author of* Alice's Adventures in Wonderland; *Andrew Kitchener, author of a well known paper on the dodo, holding a model dodo made at the Royal Scottish Museum, photographed on Ile aux Aigrettes, Mauritius; Julian Hume, English painter, whose research on the history of the dodo has added much to present day knowledge; Hugh Strickland, co-author of* The Dodo and its Kindred.

BOTTOM ROW

Masauji Hachisuka, author of The Dodo and Kindred Birds, *on an expedition to the Philippines; Alfred Newton, author of several papers on the dodo and creator of a large archive of dodo material; Edward Newton, brother of Alfred and once Colonial Secretary on Mauritius.*

and bear little relationship to the actual facts.

These two grossly eccentric works are widely quoted but they are best disregarded – or at least taken with a pinch of salt – by anyone wishing to approach dodo truth.

Nor is it just the books that are poorly written and thought through. Many papers in scientific journals are equally disappointing. S. A. Temple's paper (1977) on the dodo and the tambalacoque nut is a fine example. Temple claimed to have conceived the idea (in fact, he 'borrowed' it from a much earlier and rather more measured work by R.E. Vaughan and P.O. Wiehe (1941)) that the endemic Mauritian tambalacoque tree (*Calvaria major*) was becoming extinct simply because its seeds would not germinate without being passed through the gut of a dodo. There had been no dodos around for three centuries, he argued, and therefore all tambalacoque trees must, of necessity be more than three hundred years old. His real point was that the tree was doomed because of a special relationship with the dodo. There was not a shred of evidence to support this profound opinion, by the way, but for a while it was taken seriously.

There is a story that Temple was actually standing in a grove full of young and sprouting tambalacoque trees as he came to this grave conclusion, but his knowledge of the trees was so limited that he didn't recognize them. This may well be untrue but what can be said with certainty is that he was entirely wrong and tambalacoques can survive perfectly well without dodos. The tree is endangered but its problems are not referable to a lack of dodos.

Such is the power of the dodo to inspire myths that there are many badly-conceived ideas of this kind. The notion of a fat season and a thin one to account for discrepancies in the surviving paintings and descriptions is one of them. Many bird species have fat and thin periods but, largely because of the nature of feathering, this doesn't show visually. It is simply something that becomes evident on the weighing scales.

The calculations that have been made concerning the actual number of living birds that reached Europe are truly bizarre. Both Hachisuka and Oudemans were guilty of such speculation and some ornithologists take their findings seriously – even though they are not based on even the most minimal evidence. The means and methods by which these findings were constructed (often depending on perceived differences in paintings) are obtuse in the extreme. So too is the idea that some of the fatter, more hunched up dodo pictures result from a sitter that had been grotesquely fattened up during the long sea voyage from Mauritius and the bird had developed a terribly bent-legged posture because it was forced to travel in a box that was too small for it. Such conjecture – with absolutely nothing to base it on – is almost too ludicrous to refute. The bird appears swollen in the picture because of artistic license or incompetence, or because a badly stuffed creature served as the artist's model.

Then there is the matter of species. Hachisuka (1953) wasn't content with one species for Mauritius and another for Rodrigues (for the existence of both of which there is an abundance of proof in the shape of bones). He waxed lyrical on the subject of a third species on Réunion, for which not one scrap of hard proof has been found to prove its existence. There is, in fact, some circumstantial evidence suggesting that a dodo-like creature might once have lived on the island so perhaps he shouldn't be too heavily censored for this particular opinion. However, even this hypothetical third species wasn't quite enough for Hachisuka and he decided it would be necessary to erect a fourth to account for all the evidence – or, at least, what he perceived to be evidence. Neither Hachisuka, nor Oudemans – nor, for that matter, a number of others – were able to sift good evidence from bad and this, in itself, might seem something of a mystery.

Why should such nonsense be told about the dodo by serious men? The answer has to be because they become obsessed with the bird and, finding there is such little actual hard information, become disappointed. There then seems to be a great – and widespread – temptation (perhaps even obligation) to make things up and embellish the tale. Is it sloppy scholarship? Certainly. But perhaps it is something more. Perhaps the loss of this creature affronts people at a very deep level and there is a genuine psychological need to somehow re-invent the living bird. People want to touch the dodo and it is, of course, impossible to touch a shadow.

In Mauritius the image of the dodo is everywhere. Each shop has its own dodo product: dodo matches, dodo drinks, dodo burgers, dodo books. The image of the bird occurs on ashtrays, crockery, statuettes, tea towels, clocks etc. etc. The list is endless. There are so many dodo souvenirs on sale that one could fill a cargo ship with them. There is no sign that the dodo industry is letting up or that man's interest in the bird itself is waning.

The Solitary-Bird.

The Rodrigues Solitary

PAGE 154
Rodrigues solitary. The only known picture drawn by someone who saw the bird in life is this engraving made by François Leguat for his book A New Voyage to the East Indies *(1708).*

RIGHT
The frontispiece and title page of F. Leguat's A New Voyage to the East Indies *(1708).*

FACING PAGE
The spine of a copy of Leguat's book.

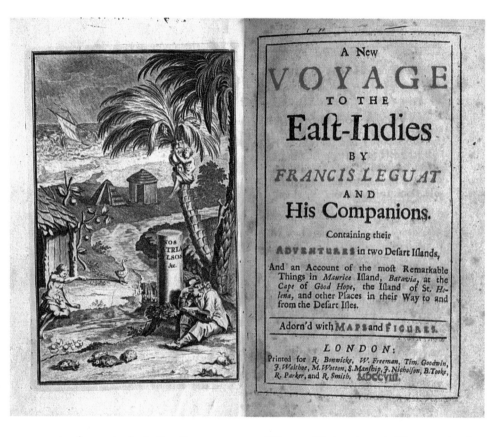

Lying far out in the Indian Ocean, some 300miles (480 km) east of Mauritius, is the tiny island of Rodrigues. Here in quiet isolation a dodo-like bird evolved from the same – or very similar – ancestral stock that generated the dodo.

The first published notice of a dodoesque bird on this remote island comes from the pen of Thomas Herbert (1634). His report is often overlooked but it speaks for itself. Of the dodo he wrote:

First here [Mauritius] *only and in Dygarrois is generated the Dodo.*

Dygarrois (Diego Ruis Island) is the name by which Rodrigues was known during the early seventeenth century. Elsewhere in his book Herbert wrote:

Dygarrois...an ile so desolate; desolate, I mean, in human inhabitants; other things 'tis uberous in, as wood (choyce and store), Tortoises, Dodos and other Fowle rare and serviceable.

Clearly, Herbert was aware that something closely akin to the dodo lived on the island. He sailed past Rodrigues but didn't land – so this particular piece of intelligence must have been passed on to him by others.

Another enigmatic early record comes from the year 1700 when Hyde made the cursory note in his book *Veterum Persarum* that dodos are chiefly to be found in 'Madagascar and Dygarroys'.

Nothing more is heard of the bird that has come to be known as the Rodrigues solitary until the year 1708 when the memoirs of a Huguenot refugee by the name of François Leguat were published under the title *A New Voyage to the East Indies* (or, in French, *Voyage et Avantures de François Leguat en Deux Isles Desertes des Indes Orientales*). Leguat's book marks the first serious notice of the solitary and the comparative lateness of this record is probably due to the fact that Rodrigues was so rarely visited.

The story of Leguat is a curious and dramatic one. Several times it has been called into question and described as a work of fiction, most famously because of several papers written by an American academic named Geoffroy Atkinson (1920, 1921 and 1922). Atkinson's disgracefully inadequate research led him to believe that Legaut never existed and that his story was made up. Ironically, the scholarship is as shoddy as that

of Hachisuka (1953) and Oudemans (1917), yet – just like these authors – his work has been given a status that it in no way merits. There can be little doubt that the story of Leguat is essentially a true one (for a masterly refutation of Atkinson's ideas *see* North-Coombes, 1979) and that, by and large, his reminiscences can be relied upon.

Leguat's tale centres around the revocation of the Edict of Nantes, which took place in 1685. This edict originally granted a certain amount of freedom of religious worship to non-catholics in France and French possessions but King Louis XIV decided its influence should be terminated. The revocation put French protestants into a dreadful predicament and many fled to neighbouring – and sympathetic – countries, most particularly Holland. Leguat seems to have been one of these unfortunates. Under the restrictions imposed by the revocation he would have lost all his possessions on leaving France and so – presumably – he arrived in Holland virtually destitute.

At some point he was put in charge of a small group of Huguenots who, fleeing from the religious persecution, were determined to settle in freedom on islands in the Indian Ocean. Accordingly, during the late summer of 1690 they left a Dutch port aboard a vessel, the *Hirondelle*, bound for the Indian Ocean. Their precise destination was the far-distant Mascarene island of Réunion, a territory they believed now abandoned by the French. Most of them (they were originally ten in number) were never to see Europe again, illness, accidental death and misadventure claiming them at various stages of the expedition. A few, including Leguat himself, did manage to get back. As the boat sailed into the waters of the North Sea, the

ABOVE LEFT
Rodrigues as it once appeared from the sea. A nineteenth century papyrograph from H. E. Strickland and A.G. Melville's The Dodo and its Kindred *(1848).*

BELOW LEFT
A picturesque cove in present-day Rodrigues.

found there. Despite the fact that his observations have been called into question and his book pronounced a hoax, much documentary evidence has come to light confirming that Leguat was exactly who he said he was and there is no reason to disbelieve his account. Certainly, the descriptions of the creatures he encountered, sometimes considered fanciful, have in several instances been supported by the discovery of skeletal material.

Leguat's best known discovery, if discovery it may be called, was the bird that he was to christen the solitary. In fact the species is often called by the name given in French editions of Leguat's book – solitaire. This name causes some confusion, however, as it has also been applied to the alleged white dodo that may once have existed on Réunion. The exact status of this creature is uncertain (see next chapter) and a dodo-like bird may indeed have given rise to the legend, although it seems more likely that an ibis was responsible.

It is perfectly obvious that Leguat was enchanted by his solitary. The lack of female companionship was obviously playing on his mind when he wrote:

They have two elevations upon the crop, of which the feathers are whiter than the rest, and which resemble, very marvelously, the beautiful bosom of a woman.

The feature is clearly shown in the picture Leguat carefully drew to illustrate his book, but the comparison is neatly sidestepped in some editions which refer instead to, 'the fine neck of a beautiful woman'.

Following the glowing comparison already made, Leguat continued:

Huguenots perhaps watched with mixed feelings as the shores of northern Europe slipped further and further behind them. Weeks later, when the intended refuge finally hove into view, any hopeful expectations were dashed, the French were still in possession, and the ship's captain changed course immediately for unoccupied Rodrigues, several hundred miles to the east. Here the refugees disembarked and were immediately abandoned by the captain, who vanished quickly over the horizon with his ship. The beleaguered group were forced to make the best of their situation and they built huts and made gardens. For two years they stayed until the hopeless loneliness and – more particularly – a lack of women, drove them to the desperate remedy of constructing a home-made boat and crossing 300 miles or so (480 km) of open sea to Mauritius.

During the years spent on Rodrigues, Leguat made detailed records of the birds he

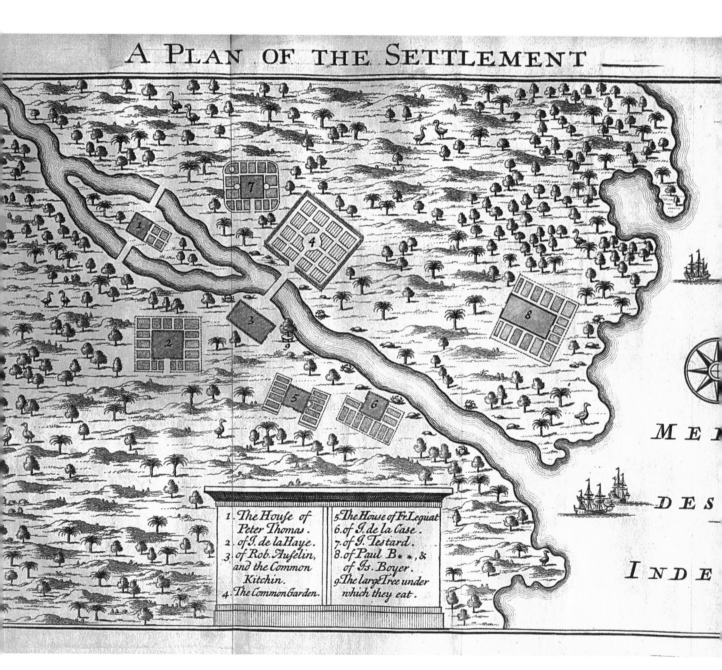

A PLAN OF THE SETTLEMENT

1. The House of Peter Thomas.
2. of J. de la Haye.
3. of Rob. Auselin, and the Common Kitchin.
4. The Common Garden.
5. The House of Fr. Leguat
6. of J. de la Case.
7. of J. Testard.
8. of Paul B✱✱, & of Is. Boyer.
9. The large Tree under which they eat.

MER

DES

INDE

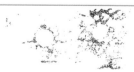

They walk with such stately form and good grace that one cannot help admiring and loving them.

Of mating and nesting he adds:

All the while they are sitting...or bringing up their young one, which is not able to provide for its self in several Months, they will not suffer any other Bird of their Species to come within 200 yards round of the place; But what is very singular, is that Males will never drive away the Females; only when he perceives one he makes a noise with his wings to call [his] *Female, and she drives the unwelcome Stranger away, not leaving it till 'tis without her Bounds. The Female do's the same as the Males, whom she leaves to the Male, and he drives them away...After these birds have rais'd their young One, and left it to its self, they are always together...and tho' they happen to mingle with other Birds of the same Species, these two Companions never disunite. We have often remark'd, that some days after the young one leaves the nest, a company of 30 or 40 brings another young one to it, and the new fledg'd Bird with its Father and Mother joyning with the Band, march to some bye Place. We frequently follow'd them, and found that afterwards the old ones went each their own way alone, or in couples, and left the two young ones together, which we called a Marriage.*

Leguat's obvious affection for them didn't stop him from enjoying roast solitary from time to time. He reported that from March to September they were plump and excellent to eat, particularly the young birds.

For Leguat himself the end of his story was ultimately a happy one although the survivors of his little band were destined to endure considerable suffering before any of them reached home. The flight from Rodrigues was only the beginning of a peculiar train of events that was to take them even further from their homeland. Soon after they successfully reached Mauritius, the Dutch Governor of the island was made aware of their arrival. After several months of deliberation on the political implications of their presence, he banished Leguat's little band to a small, rocky islet. After three years imprisoned thus, they were packed off – still prisoners – to Batavia in the Dutch East Indies, but just a year later they were released and shipped back to Holland. Here, the survivors arrived in June 1698, almost eight years after leaving, having completed a round trip of some 38,400 km (24,000 miles) during one of history's least known, most pointless, but, for all that, quite remarkable voyages.

FACING PAGE
Leguat's plan of his settlement on Rodrigues – decorated with solitarys.

BELOW
The Rodrigues solitary – a reconstruction by F.W. Frohawk. Chromolithograph from W. Rothschild's Extinct Birds (1907).

Dodo from extinction to icon

Leguat himself published his account of his travels in English and French editions in London during 1708 and there is a record that he died in England during 1735 having reached the remarkably advanced age of 97 years.

Leguat wasn't the only person to write an account of the solitary. In 1874 a discovery was made in the archives of the Ministère de la Marine, Paris. A document was found by a Mauritian magistrate who was spending some time in Paris, and this document has come to be known as the *Relation de l'Île Rodrigue*. The manuscript is anonymous although it was probably written by a man named Tafforet who was marooned on the island for several months during the year 1726. Concerning the solitary the document says:

The Solitary...weighs...40 or 50 pounds. They have a very big head, with a...frontlet, as if of black velvet. Their feathers are neither feathers nor fur...of a light grey colour, with a little black on their backs. Strutting proudly about...they preen their plumage ...and keep themselves very clean...Their toes [are] furnished with very hard scales, and [they] run with quickness...among the rocks, where a man, however agile, can hardly catch them. They have a...short beak, which is sharp... They do not fly at all, having no feathers to their wings but they flap them and make a great noise...I have never seen but one little one alone with them, and if anyone tried to approach it, they would bite him severely. These birds live on seeds and leaves of trees...I have eaten them; they are tolerably well tasted.

Long after the passing of Leguat and the anonymous author, bones were found to confirm that a bird bearing great affinity to the dodo once lived on Rodrigues. These even show nuances of detail mentioned by Leguat. Thus a 'little round mass as big as a musket ball' that the Huguenot claimed occurred on the wing, exists in skeletons as a bony knob on the metacarpal. Curiously, Leguat's mention of this unusual feature – now confirmed by bones – was one of the elements that brought his story into question as it seemed so unlikely to those without anatomical experience. In fact, such a feature occurs on the skeletons of the squabs of other pigeon species.

Skeletal material for the solitary has subsequently been found in considerable quantity, mostly in cave deposits. Several whole skeletons

FACING PAGE
Solitarys defending their territory. Acrylic on board by Julian Hume. A painting based on the account of Leguat. Reproduced by kind permission of the artist.

LEFT
A reconstruction by Julian Hume. Acrylic on paper. Collection of Cyril Walker. Reproduced by kind permission of the artist.

BELOW
Evidence of the small 'musket ball' on the bones of the wing.

exist, each of which has probably been made up from the bones of several individuals. One of the features that these reveal is an enormous sexual variation in size with male birds being much bigger than female.

During 1754 a one-time Governor of Réunion penned recollections of Rodrigues and its inhabitants. He described the solitary as being as large as a swan, with a sad face and scarcely any tail or wings, and added, 'in captivity one sees him always in the same line, no matter how much room he has, and returning the same way, without variation'. Presumably, such poor captured birds never left the Mascarenes, or perhaps not even Rodrigues. As far as is known, none was ever brought to Europe.

Although the species seems to have been still common enough during the 1720s, it

RIGHT
Male and female Rodrigues solitary skeletons – collected in 1874 by the Rev. H.H. Slater – in The Hunterian Museum, Royal College of Surgeons, London.

FACING PAGE
Bones from a Rodrigues solitary, showing their great similarity to those of a dodo. Lithograph by J. Dinkel from H. E. Strickland and A. G. Melville's The Dodo and its Kindred *(1848).*

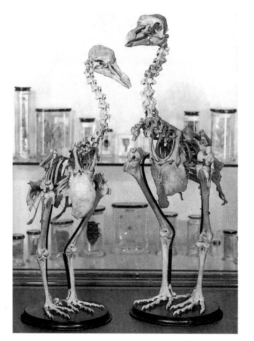

must have declined rapidly after this. During 1761 the Abbé Pingré made the long trip from France to Rodrigues to observe the transit of Venus. He arrived in time to see the wonder in the heavens but not in time to see the solitary – although he was assured that individuals still lived. One little footnote to the Abbé's adventure is that a friend of his, the French astronomer Pierre Charles le Monnier, placed the bird itself in the heavens to commemorate the Abbé's mission. Le Monnier borrowed a few faint stars from Libra and the tail of Hydra in honour of the expedition. Since celestial mapmakers had no idea what the solitary looked like, star maps show it first as the solitary thrush of the Philippines and later as an owl. After 1825 the idea seems to have fallen into disuse. The solitary, then, has the unique claim among extinct birds of being an astronomical object.

During 1831 a resident of the island for some 40 years maintained that he had never seen a bird large enough to be a solitary so it seems fairly certain that the species died out during the second half of the eighteenth century. Rodrigues has an area of only 104 square km (40 sq. miles) and it is unlikely that such large birds could survive there for long without being detected.

Rodrigues solitarys were, perhaps, primarily birds of the woods – not, it seems, the shores – and here they fed on dates (according to Leguat) or seeds and leaves (according to the anonymous author). Although their only defense was a nasty bite and their wings were useless for flight, they don't seem to have fallen prey to man very easily. But there is little doubt that they were caught, and caught often. When that happened, they made no sound. According to Leguat, they simply – 'shed tears'.

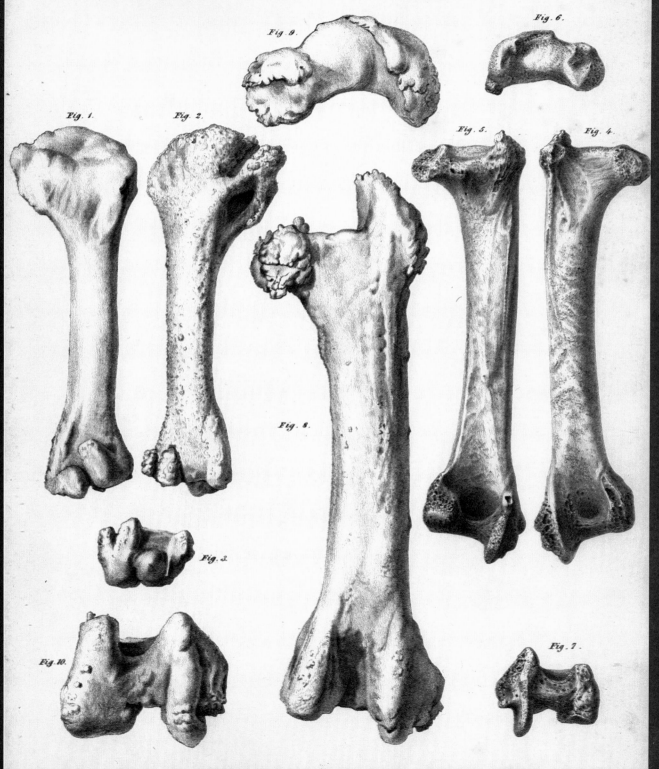

Plate XIV.

Fig. 9.

Fig. 6.

Fig. 1.

Fig. 2.

Fig. 5.

Fig. 4.

Fig. 8.

Fig. 3.

Fig. 10.

Fig. 7.

DIDUS SOLITARIUS

(One-Third Natural Size—*from a Dutch picture taken from living bird in Amsterdam, beak and wing restored*)

The White Dodo
of Réunion

The White Dodo of Réunion

PAGE 166
White dodo – a reconstruction. Chromolithograph by F. W. Frohawk from W. Rothschild's Extinct Birds *(1907).*

FACING PAGE
White Dodo with other Birds. *Watercolour by Pieter Withoos. The Natural History Museum, London.*

Whether or not there was ever a dodo-like bird inhabiting the island of Réunion is one of the little mysteries of ornithology. There is some very thin evidence to show that there might have been but it is too flimsy to make much of. With a dodo on Mauritius and the dodo-like solitary on Rodrigues, it might seem reasonable to suppose that a similar species once lived on Réunion, the third Mascarene island. Yet not a single piece of bone has been recovered from deposits on the island to establish this and put the matter beyond doubt.

There are four written accounts that might relate to such a bird. The earliest is by V. I. Bontekoe who visited Réunion around 1619 but whose memoirs were not published until 1646. This lapse may be significant. Who knows what Bontekoe may have forgotten or confused during the intervening time?

There were also some Dod-eersen, which had small wings but could not fly; they were so fat they could scarcely walk, for when they walked their belly dragged along the ground.

J. Tatton, who wrote in 1625, said:

A great fowl the bigness of a Turkie, very fat, and so short-winged that they cannot flie, beeing white, and in a manner tame; and so are all other fowles as having not been troubled or feared with shot.

What did these men see? The descriptions seem to indicate dodos or dodoesque birds. But even if both men were actually describing dodos, it is just possible that they saw individuals that had been taken from Mauritius to Réunion. Yet Tatton clearly says that the birds he saw were white and this whiteness has introduced another element to the story. There are four (perhaps five) seventeenth century pictures that show, unequivocally, a white dodo and, perhaps understandably, several writers have suggested that these pictures show the white dodo of Réunion. More probably they show an albinistic individual of the regular kind or they are works that show considerable artistic licence. We have no idea of the intentions of the artists involved and they may have produced 'white dodos' simply because they wanted to. In other words the pictures could have been painted purely for decorative effect.

Although there are several white dodo paintings, in terms of analysis they may be regarded as one. All are related works. Indeed, three of them are virtually identical. These were painted by Pieter Holsteyn – or perhaps his son – during the 1630s (there is a slim chance they may have been painted a few years later). A fourth, by Pieter Withoos, produced some years after the Holsteyn ones, is clearly based on the earlier pictures. The Withoos painting (a variant once existed but can no longer be traced) and those by Holsteyn show the same strange arrangement of the wing feathers and a peculiar deformity of the beak. Only one of these pictures can truly be considered an 'original' image; the

White Dodo.
Watercolour (probably painted during the 1630s) by Pieter Holsteyn. Two other pictures by Holsteyn are virtually identical to this one (see illustration on facing page). Teylers Museum, Haarlem.

rest are simply copies.

The argument (often put forward by ornithologists) that the Withoos picture must show an accurately painted dodo as the other figured birds are so realistically shown, does not stand up to examination. A dodo, directly copied from the earlier Holsteyn paintings, has simply been inserted into a landscape filled with more common birds – leaving us no way of judging the accuracy, or otherwise, of the original image.

Whether the pictures show a genuine albinistic dodo or whether they are more imaginative works, there is nothing to link them with Réunion apart, of course, from the word 'white'.

There are two more written descriptions that were once considered to relate to a Réunion dodo, but these two are much later than the other pair. The first of these was given by the traveller M. Dubois during 1674.

Dubois gave a number of enigmatic descriptions of birds he saw and this, unfortunately, is as difficult to interpret as any of the others:

These birds are so called [solitaires] *because they always go alone. They are as big as a large goose and have white plumage with the tips of the wings and tail black. The tail*

A second picture by Pieter Holsteyn, clearly derived from the same source. This painting was once in the collection of Baron van der Feltz of Amsterdam but its present whereabouts have not been determined.

feathers are like those of the ostrich, they have a long neck and...legs and feet like a turkey. This bird is caught by running after it, since it can scarcely be said to fly at all.

The second of these later reports was written by M. Carré (1699):

I saw a kind of bird in this place which I have not found elsewhere; it is that which the inhabitants call the Oiseaux Solitaire for to be sure, it loves solitude and only frequents the most secluded places; one never sees two or more together; it is always alone. It is not unlike a turkey, if it did not have longer legs. The beauty of its plumage is a delight to see. It is of changeable colour which verges upon yellow.

These two enigmatic accounts were long associated with the idea of a dodo but recently it has become more attractive to associate them with an ibis, bones of which have now been found on Réunion. The tail feathers looking somewhat like those of an ostrich is a description perhaps suggestive of the rather disintegrated feathering of a sacred ibis (*Threskiornis aethiopicus*) which is, after all, an inhabitant of (nearby!) Madagascar. The white plumage with tips of the wing and tail black, the long neck and legs might also

The White Dodo of Réunion

FACING PAGE

The Réunion ibis – a creature that may have had some influence on the legend of a dodo on the island. The bird is known only from bones so this reconstruction shows its presumed appearance in life and its probable similarity to the sacred ibis. Acrylic on paper by Julian Hume. Reproduced by kind permission of the artist.

suggest this species. The sacred ibis also has white feathers that merge into yellow.

The provable fact that ibises were once on Réunion has been used to entirely negate the idea of a dodo. It does nothing of the sort, of course. The finding of ibis bones simply proves that ibises once lived there. It has little bearing on whatever else may have done. Although such finds may cloud the issue – or even make the possibility of the former existence of a dodo less likely – they certainly don't disprove it.

As far as the Réunion dodo is concerned, it can only be said that it is *possible* that such a creature once existed. There is a *small* – very small – amount of evidence to suggest it might have done, but until such time as skeletal material is uncovered, the creature must be considered mythical.

One other point may be worth making. The various recreations of white dodos that have been commissioned by dodo enthusiasts (Rothschild, Hachisuka etc.) very much miss the point. If a dodo-like creature did, in fact, once inhabit Réunion it would certainly not have looked exactly like a regular dodo, with the only major difference lying in the coloration of the plumage. Any creature evolving on Réunion would have been evolving – once it had lost the power of flight – in complete isolation. It would, therefore, have followed a rather different line to that pursued by the dodo of Mauritius and would certainly have acquired a number of independant features. Just as the solitary of Rodrigues evolved in isolation to become a markedly different creature to the dodo, so too would any dodoesque bird on Réunion have developed in a distinctive way. It would certainly not have developed into a creature that looked exactly the same as its relative.

The assumption that it did derives solely from the pictures of Pieter Holsteyn and it is clear that these paintings – whatever their true nature may be – have nothing to do with Réunion.

A curious footnote to the tale lies in a record (found by Hachisuka (1953)) that suggests that dodos (or ibises) were still living while M. de la Bourdonnaye – one of the most important figures in the history of Mauritius – was Governor of Mauritius and Réunion; this was between the years 1735 and 1746. M. de la Bourdonnaye is, in fact, supposed to have sent a dodo from Réunion back to France. If it ever arrived, and what subsequently became of it, is not known. Any such creature may have been a Rodrigues solitary, of course.

Acknowledgements

The author would like to thank Julian Hume for sharing much of his knowledge of Mauritius and for permission to reproduce his paintings, Rungwe Kingdon, Bob Thorneycroft and Andrew Kitchener for help of various kinds, Carl Jones for advice and hospitality in Mauritius, Rob Chinery for photos, Peter Southon, Christine Jackson and Ralfe Whistler for regularly drawing attention to interesting and curious items.

The Last Chance.
Wood engraving by Colin See-Paynton. Reproduced by kind permission of the artist.

Saftleven's Dodo,
imagined by Errol Fuller.
Oils on panel.

Bibliography

Anonymous. 1599. *A True Report of the gainefull, prosperous and speedy voyage to Java in the East Indies.* London.

Anonymous. 1601. *Het Tvveede Boeck. Journael oft Dagh-register, inhoudende een warachtich verhael ende Historische Vertellinghe van de reyse, gedaen door de achte schepen van Amstelredamme gheseylt inden Maent Martij 1598, onder 'theleydt van den Admiral Jacob Cornelisz. Neck, ende Wybrant Van Varvvijck als Vice-Admirael.* Amsterdam.

Anonymous. 1646. *Begin ende Voortgang vande Vereenigde Neederlantsch Geoctroyeer de Oost-Indische Campagnie, vervattende de Voornaemste Reysen.* Amsterdam.

Anonymous. 1656. *Museum Tradescantium, or a collection of rarities preserved at South-Lambeth near London by John Tradescant.* London.

Anonymous. 1669. *Orientalische Reise Beschreibunge...Jurgen Andersen aus Schleswig und Volquard Iversen aus Holstein.* Schleswig.

Atkinson, G. 1920. *The Extraordinary Voyage in French Literature before 1700.* Paris.

Atkinson, G. 1921. The French Desert Novel of 1708. *Publi. Modern Land Ass. of America*, vol. 26.

Atkinson, G. 1922. *The Extraordinary Voyage in French Literature from 1700-1720.* Paris.

Blainville, H. D. 1829. Memoire sur le Dodo. *Nouv. Ann. du Musee d'Hist. Nat.*, 4, pp.1-46.

Blainville, H. D. 1835. Memoire sur le Dodo, autrement Dronte. *Nouv. Ann. Mus.*, vol. 4, pp.1-36.

Bontekoe van Hoorn. 1650. *Iovrnael ofte Gedenckwaerdige beschrijvinghe vande Oost-Indische Reyse van Villem Ijsbrantsz. Bontekoe van Hoorn.* Amsterdam.

Brown, Sir T. 1836. *Works* (Wilkens Edition) – contains Sir Hamon L'Estrange's account. London.

Carré. M. 1699. *Voyage des Indes Orientales.* Paris.

Carroll, L. 1865. *Alice's Adventures in Wonderland.* Oxford: Clarendon Press.

Cauche, F. 1651. *Relations veritables et curieuses de l'Isle de Madagascar et du Bresil.* Paris.

Cheke, A (1987) – *see* Diamond, A.W.

Cheke, A., Gardner, T., Jones, C., Owadally, A. and

Staub, F. 1984. Did the Dodo do it? *Animal Kingdom*, 87 (1), pp. 4–6.

Clark, G. 1865. Account of the late discovery of Dodo remains in the island of Mauritius. *Ibis*, pp.141–146.

Clusius, C. A. 1605. *Exoticorum Libri Decem.* Antwerp.

De Bry, T & J.J. 1601. *Variorum Navigatornis.* Tom. 1. Frankfurt.

Diamond, A.W. 1987. *Studies of Mascarene Island Birds.* Cambridge: University Press.

Dubois, Pere. 1674. *Les Voyages faits par le Seiur D.B. aux Isles Dauphine ou Madagascar, et Bourbon ou Mascarenne.* Paris.

Duncan, J. S. 1828. A summary review of the authorities on which naturalists are justified in believing that the dodo was a bird existing in the Isle of France. *Zoological Journal*, vol.3, pp.554–567.

Edwards, G. 1760. *Gleanings of Natural History.* London.

Frauenfeld, G. von. 1868. *Neu aufgefundene Abbildung des Dronte und eines zweiten kurzflugeligen Vogels, wahrwcheinlich des "Poule rouge au bec de becasse" der Maskarenen in der Privatbibliothek S. M. des verstorbenen Kaiser Franz.* Vienna.

Fuller, E. 2000. *Extinct Birds.* Oxford: University Press.

Greenway, J. 1958. *Extinct and Vanishing Birds of the World.* New York.

Grew, N. 1681. *Museum Regalis Societatis.* London.

Gunther, R. 1937. The Oxford Dodos. *Bird Notes and News*, vol.17, no.6, pp.141–2.

Hachisuka, M. 1937. Revisional Note on the Didine Birds of Reunion. *Proc. Biol. soc. Washington*, vol.1, pp.69–72.

Hachisuka, M. 1953. *The Dodo and Kindred Birds.* London: Witherby.

Herbert, Sir T. 1634. *A Relation of some yeares' Travaile, begunne Anno 1626, into Afrique and the greater Asia, especially the territories of the Persian Monarchie, and some parts of the oriental Indies and Isles adiacent.* London: T. H. Esquier.

Hume, J. (in prep.) The Journal of the Flagship Gelderland – Dodo and other birds on Mauritius 1601. *Archives of Natural History* (2002?).

Hyde. 1700. *Veterum Persarum et Parthorum et Medorum Religionis Historia.* Oxford.

Killermann, S. 1915. Die ausgestorbenen Maskarenvogel, mit 15 davon einigen neu aufgefundenen Abbildungen. *Naturwissenschaftliche Wochenschrift*, (June 1915), pp.353–360, p.369.

Kitchener, A. 1993. Justice at last for the dodo. *New Scientist* (August 28th 1993).

Kitchener, A. 1993. On the external appearance of the dodo. *Archives of Natural History*, 20 (2), pp.279–301.

Latimer, M. C. 1953. A Dodo Egg. *Suid Africaanse Joernaal van Wetenskap*, vol.49, no.6 (January, 1953), p.208-210.

Leguat. F. 1708. *Voyages et Aventures de Francois Leguat & de ses Campagnons, en deux isles desertes des Indes Orientales*. London: David Mortier.

Leguat, F. 1708. *A New Voyage to the East Indies*. London: R. Bonwick.

Livezey, B.C. 1993. An encomorphological review of the dodo and solitaire. *J. Zool. London*, pp. 274–292.

Michel, C. 1992. *Birds of Mauritius*. Port Louis: Editions de l'ocean Indien.

Moree, P. 2001. *Dodo's en galjoenen*. Zutphen: Walburg Pers.

Moreau, C. 1999. *Le Solitaire de l'ile Rodrigues*. Port Mathurin, Rodrigues.

Mourer-Chauviré, C., Bour, R and Ribes, S. 1995. Position systématique du Solitaire de la Réunion: nouvelle interprétation basée sur les restes fossiles et les récits des anciens voyageurs. *C.R. Acad. Sci. Paris*, t. 320, série II a, pp.1125–1131.

Mundy, P. *see* Temple, R. and Anstey, L.

Newton, A. 1865. Notes of a visit to Rodrigues. *Ibis*, p.146.

Newton, A. 1868. Note on unpublished figures of the dodo and other birds of Mauritius. *Ibis*, pp. 503-504.

Newton, A. 1868. On the Osteology of the Solitaire or Didine Bird of the Island of Rodrigues. *Phil. Trans. Royal Soc. London*, vol. clix, pp.327–362.

Newton, A. 1874. On a Living Dodo shipped for England in the year 1628. *Proc. Zool. Soc. London*, pp.307, 447–449.

Newton, E. 1868. Discovery of Didus solitarius. *Trans. Roy. Soc. Arts. Sc. Mauritius*, new series, 3, pp.31–38.

Newton, E. and Gadow, H. 1893. On additional bones of the Dodo and other extinct birds of Mauritius obtained by Mr. Theodore Sauzier. *Trans. Zool. Soc., London*, vol. 13, pp. 281–302.

Nieuhof, J. 1682. *Nieuhofs gedenkweerdige zeeen lantreize door de voormrnaemste Landschappen van West en Oostindien*. Amsterdam.

North-Coombes, A. 1979. *The Vindication of François Leguat*. Port Louis: Service Bureau.

Olearius, A. 1666. *Beschreibung der gottorfischen Kunstkammer*. Copenhagen.

Oudemans, A. C. 1917. *Dodo-Studien*. Amsterdam: Johannes Muller.

Owadally, A. 1979. The Dodo and the Tambalacoque Tree. *Science*, vol.23 (March 30th).

Owen, R. 1849. Observations on the Dodo. *Trans. Zool. Soc. London*, vol 3. pp.331–338.

Owen, R. 1866. *Memoir on the Dodo, with an Historical Introduction by the late Wm. J. Broderip*. London: Taylor and Francis.

Owen, R. On the Osteology of the Dodo. *Trans, Zool. Soc., London*, vol. 6, pp.49–55.

Owen, R. 1872. On the Dodo (part II). *Trans. Zool. Soc., London*, vol. 7, pp.513–525.

Owen, R. 1879. *Memoirs on theExtinct Wingless Birds of New Zealand; with an Appendix on those of England, Australia, Newfoundland, Mauritius and Rodrigues*. London: Jan Van Voorst.

Pine, G. 1668. *The Isle of Pines*. London: T. Cadell.

Pitot, A. 1905. *T'Eylandt Mauritius*. Port Louis: Coignet Freres.

Pitot, A. 1914. Extinct Birds of the Mauritian Island (appendix to *Mauritius Illustrated*). London.

Quammen, D. 1996. *The Song of the Dodo*. London: Hutchinson.

Reinhardt, J. 1842. Nojere Oplysning om det i Kjoben-havn funde Dronte hoved. *Naturh. Tidskr.* vol. 4, pp.71–72.

Reinhardt, J. 1843. Genauere Erklarung uber den in Kopenhagen gefundenen Drontenkopf. *Isis von Oken*, p.58.

Rothschild, W. 1907. *Extinct Birds*. London: Hutchinson.

Rothschild, W. 1919. On one of four original pictures from life of the Réunion or White Dodo. *Ibis*, pp.78–79.

Shaw, G. and Nodder. F. 1789–1813. *Naturalist's Miscellany*, 24 vols (dodo accounts are in vols. 4 and 5). London.

Soeteboom, H. (ed.). 1648. *Deerde voornaemste Zee-gettogt na de Oost-Indien: gedaan met de Achinsche en Moluksche vloten, onder de Admmiralen Jacob Hemskerk en Wolfert Harmanszoon. In den jare 1601, 1602, 1603.* Amsterdam.

Staub, F. 1993. *Fauna de l'ile Maurice et Flora Associee.* Mauritius.

Staub, F. 1996. Dodos and Solitaires, Myths and Reality. *Proceedings of the Royal Society of Arts and Sciences of Mauritius*, vol. 6, pp.89–122.

Sterland, W. J. 1867. The White Dodo. *Science Gossip*, p.5.

Strickland, H. E. and Melville, A.G. 1848. *The Dodo and its Kindred.* London: Benham, Reeves.

Tatton, J. 1625. *Voyage of Castleton (1613)* in *Purchas's Pilgrimage*, vol. 1. London.

Temple, R.C. and Anstey, L.M. (eds.) 1919–36. *The Travels of Peter Mundy in Europe and Asia, 1608 –1667.* London: Haklyut Society.

Temple, S. 1977. Plant-Animal Mutualis: Coevolution with dodo Leads to Near Extinction of Plant. *Science*, vol. 197 (August 26th).

Van den Broecke, P. 1665. *Vilf verscheyde Journalen van Pieter van den Broecke.* Amsterdam.

Vaughan, R. and Wiehe, O. 1937. Studies on the vegetation of Mauritius, Part 1. *Journal of Ecology*, vol. 25.

Vaughan, R. and Wiehe, O. 1941. Studies on the vegetation of Mauritius, Part 3. *Journal of Ecology*, vol. 29.

Verkens, J. (ed.) 1613. *Eylffter Schiffahrt ander Teil od Kurtzer Verfolg u. Continhuierung der Reyse, so von den Holl. u. Seelandern in die Ost Indien mit neun grossen u. vier kleinen Schiffen von 1607 bis in das 1612 Jahr unter der Admiralschafft Peter Wilhelm Verhuffen.* Frankfurt.

West-Zanen, W. van. 1648 (*see* Soeteboom, H.)

Wissen, B van. 1995. *Dodo.* Amsterdam: Zoologisch Museum, University of Amsterdam.

Ziswiler, V. 1996. *Der Dodo - Fantasien und Fakten zu einem verschwundenen Vogel.* Zurich: Zoological Museum.

Frankie's Dodo.
The dodo as drawn by a five year old.

Index

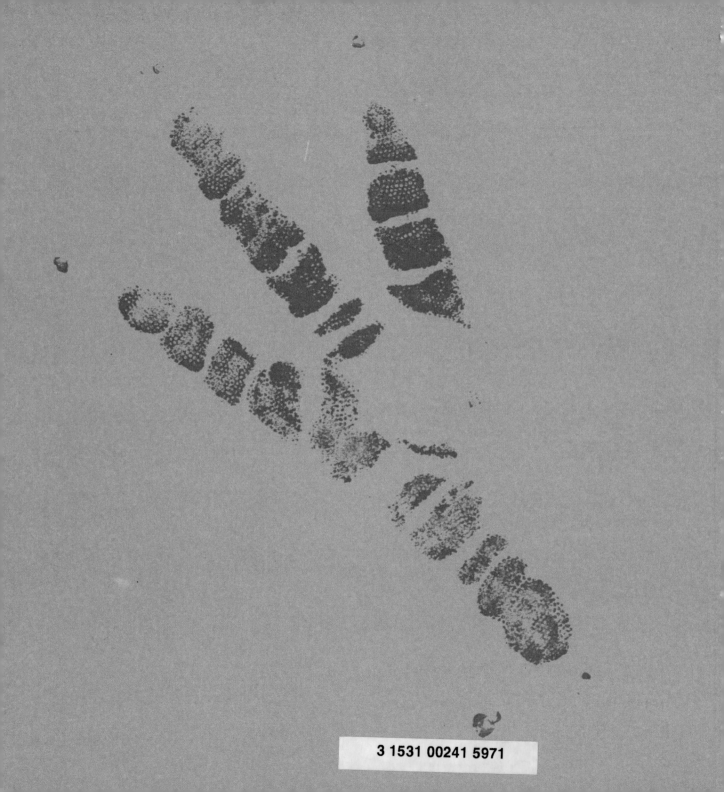

3 1531 00241 5971